Stones of Remembrance

JOURNALING GOD'S FAITHFULNESS

Jann Gray

Lumenstar Publishing™, Inc
NASHVILLE, TN

Jann Gray/ Lumenstar Publishing™, Inc (a division of PointActive, LLC)
PO Box 24625
Nashville, TN 37202
615-773-1234
www.LumenstarPublishing.com

Scripture quotations noted as ESV are from The Holy Bible, English Standard Version, copyright 2001 by Crossway, a publishing ministry of Good News Publishing

Scripture quotations noted as NLT are from The Holy Bible, New Living Translation, copyright 1996, 2004, 2015 by Tyndale House Publishing

Scripture quotations noted as NIV are from The Holy Bible, New International Version, copyright 1973, 1978, 1984, 2011 by Biblica, Inc All rights reserved worldwide.

All artwork is the work of Jann Gray unless noted otherwise.

Library of Congress Cataloging-in-Publication Data

Stones of Remembrance/ Jann Gray. —1st ed.
ISBN 978-1-5323-4221-9

Contents

i

We will tell the next generation
the praiseworthy deeds of the Lord,
His power, and the wonders He has done.

—PSALM 78:4

Dedication

To three precious women in my life who have taught me to value God's Word above all else, to hide it in my heart and to draw on it's truth, wisdom and strength on a daily basis.

I want to be like you when I grow up!

Ruth Jane Rice, (aka Jammy Jane) – Grandmother

Robyn Elizabeth Bush – Sister

Mona Corley – Friend

Acknowledgments

I have learned that writing a book is a lonely activity that is best accomplished with a small crowd of amazing and talented people. Words are inadequate to express my gratitude—but the words I express now come from a full and overflowing heart for those who have gathered around me and lent me their support and skills.

Every author should be so fortunate to have an editor who enters into the perfecting process with her in a way that adds polish to her words and joy to her heart. John Driver, you have amazed me with your insight and kindness. I am a better writer for your assistance and I couldn't have done this without you. I thank you for all the ways you enhanced my words while helping me stay true to what I wanted to say.

Deborah Jackson, you have always challenged me to expand my world beyond the experiences that are within my immediate grasp. You have a unique ability to look far down a road and yet pay attention to the details that are immediately in front of you. Thank you for sharing both of those abilities with me and being my final proof editor.

Much of the research and planning for this book was accomplished while I was on the road teaching *Illuminated Journaling Workshops*. The participants in my Workshops provided me a constant source of inspiration and motivation. I am grateful to the bookstores, churches and art studios that invited me to come share Bible Journaling with their members and customers. It was their enthusiasm, questions and encouragement that energized me to go back to my hotel room each night and spend a few hours working before putting my head on my pillow. I do not regret the lost sleep one bit!

One of those Workshop participants has played a special role in the process of writing this book. I met Melissa Gross and her friend, Thayer Bentley, at a Workshop I led at the church where I grew up in Dallas, Texas. She and Bentley were already avid Bible Journalers and we became friends quickly, the way one can when you all love Jesus and God's Word. Melissa teaches Bible Journaling too and I asked her to read the manuscript and make sure that I was including the information that people who are new to journaling need to know to be successful. She has provided valuable insight along the way and I am so blessed that she said yes.

Realtors will tell you that when it comes to buying or selling a home that the key is "location, location, location." I will tell you that when it comes to writing, location can be of equal importance. I was blessed to get to spend extended time writing at Falls Creek Falls State Park in Tennessee. The views were serene and provided the perfect backdrop for contemplating God's Word and capturing my thoughts. I am grateful to the staff that was always there for a short conversation, a word of encouragement or a moment of shared laughter. I could not have asked for a better place to step away from the distractions of every day life and concentrate solely on what God wanted me to write in this book. I do actually want to return soon to the park so I can fully enjoy all that it has to offer.

It is often small things that can derail progress in the blink of an eye. For me, the thing that was almost my undoing on this project was a power cord. Yes, if one is a writer these days, you need a computer—and that computer inevitably needs a power cord. When I first arrived at Falls Creek Falls State Park, one of the things I liked best was how far away from civilization it was. I wanted to focus on writing and nothing else and the closest town was 30 minutes away down the mountain. As I was setting up my desk, I noticed that my computer cord no longer had a light on indicating that it was charging my computer. I tried plugging it into another outlet—still no light. On closer inspection, the cord had clearly been chewed on by a puppy that will remain nameless and was beyond repair. I needed a new cord, and where was I going to find a power cord on the top of a mountain? A MacBook power cord isn't something you find at a General Store among the sweatshirts and souvenirs. But the wonderful staff at the park pointed me in the right direction. Down the mountain I went to a shop called *Computer Doctors* in Sparta, Tennessee. Chris Sapp was the owner and my hero that day. A new cord could be ordered, but would take two to three days—however, Chris had another solution. He went back into his workroom and brought out the cord that he kept on his workbench. His generosity kept me from making a longer trip to a larger town—or twiddling my thumbs back at the park while waiting for a delivery truck. Thirty minutes later, I was back at the park and the project was back on track. Sometimes it is the small things that make a big difference in our lives. Thank you Chris!

Friends and family are the backbone of my support system. I am grateful for all of the messages, texts, Facebook and Instagram comments that let me know that they were thinking and praying for me. As frustrated as I can be with the phenomenon of social media, I must confess that I am equally grateful that the technology allowed me to feel connected even while I was separated by miles from those that I love. It reminds me that most things are a two-sided coin.

Royce B. Gray, I couldn't have written one word without your support. You looked for ways to make this book happen and solved problems without me ever knowing they existed. You have made me laugh, let me cry, listened when I needed to process my thoughts and provided me with random words you thought might be helpful. If you read the *Stone of Wisdom* chapter, you will find your fingerprints all over it and more than a couple of those "random" words! You are a rare gift and I love you with all my heart!

Years ago, God gave me one of the best friends a girl could ever have—and let her be my sister too! Robyn, I know that this year has brought a journey that you would never have chosen for yourself and your children. I am so very proud of the way you have embraced the journey and rested upon the grace and mercies of God to carry you along without your husband at your side. I appreciate that even in the midst of your own challenges, you have always been there to be my sounding board and cheerleader. I love you a bushel and a peck and a hug around the neck.

A Note From Josh McDowell

As a nineteen year old college student, I was a skeptic regarding the existence of God and was convinced that the Bible couldn't possibly be a reliable source of Truth. When I was challenged to intellectually examine the claims of Christianity, I initially set out to prove that today's Bible is nothing more than a collection of distorted and unreliable records of historical and mythical events. I reasoned that if we couldn't trust that the writings of Scripture had been accurately handed down over the centuries, we would have no basis for the truth claims of the Bible. If the Bible isn't a reliable document of history, then it would be impossible to assert that it is the power-filled Word of God.

I spent months on my quest to disprove the reliability of scripture, but in the end I simply couldn't reach that conclusion. I became convinced beyond a reasonable doubt that Scripture is reliable and its very words are God's own and have real power. I've devoted the rest of my life to helping others come to that important belief as well.

I don't want anyone to have a dry or detached relationship with God and His Word. I want them to become so convinced that it is the best source of knowing God and His plans for us that they will begin to live a life empowered by the truths that they find there.

When Dottie and I first met Jann, she was a teenager with a love for God and His Word that was anything but dry or detached! Later she joined our ministry and work with us for more than 25 years to help reach young people with the life-changing truth of how to have a personal relationship with Jesus Christ. One of Jann's greatest gifts is her ability to tell a story that is both intriguing and compelling. When Jann finishes describing an event to you, you will think you were there with her. She helped thousands of our ministry partners feel like they had been right there with us when young people's lives were changed for eternity both here in the states and in Russia and Eastern Europe.

It comes as no surprise that Jann is taking the lead in helping others share their stories of what God has done in their life with those they love the most.

Second only to beginning your own personal relationship with Jesus is the job of sharing how God and His Word have changed your life with your children and others whom you love. *Legacy Journaling* is such a unique way for you to communicate the faithfulness of God to future generations.

As you read **Stones of Remembrance**, you will be equipped to communicate your personal stories in a compelling manner that will impact the hearts and minds of those for whom you created it. Your personal testimony of how you have encountered God in His Word is powerful—in fact it is *the most powerful influence* there is in persuading others to consider the claims of Christ. Just as God commanded Joshua and the people of Israel to set up a memorial of stones when they crossed into the Promised Land, your Legacy Bible will stand as a memorial of God's faithfulness in the life of your family. When your children ask, "is there power in the Word of God," this memorial Bible that Jann will help you create will share with them the compelling story of exactly how powerful it has been.

I have no doubt that the Legacy Bible that you create will become a family heirloom and treasure for this generation and for those yet to come. God's Word is trustworthy. It contains power for living like no other book. You could not give a better gift to those whom you love.

You know what He's done for you, now you just need tell the story!

Josh McDowell

Do You Remember Family Bibles?

epending upon your age, you are probably either nodding your head affirmatively or turning it a little sideways like a dog who has just detected an unfamiliar sound. Back in the day before technology made it possible to instantly search one's family lineage on sites like Ancestry.com, families actually kept real, personal records of marriages, births and deaths in their family Bibles. These Bibles were usually displayed prominently in the home and were typically much larger and more ornate than the personal Bibles one would use for everyday reading and studying.

The family Bible was passed down from one generation to the next as a way of reminding every member that, "this is our family."

As a little girl, I was fascinated by the family Bible displayed in the home of my mother's parents. I wasn't very concerned with our family's lineage at the time, but there are two thoughts I had about that Bible that have remained with me to this day. The first was that **God's Word was very important to Gramps and Jammy Jane** [the names I used for my grandparents]. Secondly, I remember feeling that there were secret wonders stowed away like hidden treasure in the pages of that Bible . . . and I just knew they could be mine if I would only spend the time to unlock them.

I think my grandparents would be pleased to know the influence their family Bible still has on my life today.

Whether you are the first in your family to become a follower of Christ or whether you come from a family of faith whose lineage dates back hundreds of years, a love for God's Word is something we all desire to pass along to future generations.

There are many obstacles to "passing the love forward" in today's culture, not the least of which is the fact that so much of our communication is done in the intangible world of texts, emojis, tweets and other social media platforms. This is not necessarily a bad thing. We are talking to one another more, we can "follow" family and friends to keep up with what is going on in their lives, and we can share in a few words what is important to us— right now.

The downside is that we often share and hear that which is more *immediate* rather than that which is more *significant*— the topics and events from our days that really affect those whom we love. Don't get me wrong . . . I *love* social media! I know more about what is going on in the lives of my son, nieces and nephew than I would ever get to know otherwise. I am admittedly a bit obsessed with *Pinterest* and I love the inspiration I find just scrolling through *Instagram*.

But the truth is, most of these platforms are more about instant communication (both for the one who posts and the one who reads) than long-term relational communication. For goodness' sakes, I follow several hundred people just on *Instagram* alone! I honestly can say that I like most of them, am inspired by many of them, am provoked to thought by a few of them . . . but I actually only *know* maybe two or three of them. And the same can be said of those that follow me. I love the opportunity to share what I am thinking and working on *that day* with several hundred encouraging folks; it is a lovely form of communication. It just isn't the best way, in my opinion, to pass on the important stuff to those who will come behind us.

I'm talking about heirloom-quality communication. I'm talking about the kinds of things you want anyone who is important to you to know. These kinds of things require more than 140 characters. They take intentionality and a bit of thought.

And that is what this book is all about—*legacy journaling*.

I want to help you find a way to communicate to those you love the things that are most important to you.

When I first discovered Bible journaling, I immediately sensed how important it was going to be to my own relationship with God. I have loved studying God's Word as a way to get to know Him for many years, but Bible Journaling, or *Illuminated Journaling* as I like to call it, has allowed me to *respond* to what I learn in a more consistent way. In my first book, **Illuminated Journaling**, I talk about how important the response component is to the learning process. It is what closes the loop for us. The learning process begins when we *read* a passage, moves forward when we *reflect* on what we have read, but is only complete when we r*espond* to what we have learned.

You probably already know this, but if you are unfamiliar with the idea of Bible journaling, it is the process of using a wide margin Bible to add text, imagery and journaling directly onto the pages you have been studying. It can be simple or elaborate; contain brightly colored or monochromatic elements; be done in pen, pencil, paint, stickers or all other sorts of mediums; or be composed of just words, just images or a combination of the two. There really aren't any rules. Most importantly, it is very personal because it is a reflection of the person doing the journaling and their unique relationship with God.

And that is the reason I have come to believe that this journaling method can be so helpful to us as we seek to share life's most important message with the people who matter to us most. I have personally begun several of these Bibles for our family. One is more of an overarching *family* Bible, another is for my son, while others are for my nieces and nephew. I have also gifted journaling Bibles to several new brides and mothers so they can begin their own legacy journaling for their families.

Whether you want to create a single *family* Bible, or one or more other Bibles for particular individuals, I hope to walk you through the process I have used for the last couple of years and offer you various ideas to consider as you figure out your own process along the way. This book is all about the *"why"* and *"what to journal"* aspects of legacy journaling. If you are also interested in a resource that will give you lots of tips, tricks, techniques and journaling prompts—a bit more of the *"how"* of journaling that you can use as you work on your own projects—let me encourage you to check out a companion to this book, the ***Stones of Remembrance Workbook***.

I love the idea of reestablishing the use of a family Bible, making it creatively relevant to the way we live our lives today. I am immensely honored and excited that you are on this journey with me and I can't wait to get started . . .

So let's begin.

In the future, when your children ask you, What do these stones mean?' tell them that these stones are to be a memorial to the people of Israel forever."

Joshua 4:6,7

CHAPTER 1

When Your Children Ask

I f ever there were an event to be memorialized in some sort of way that would span generations, it would have to be the day the Israelites crossed over the Jordan River into the land God had promised them.

This was a day that had been a long time coming!

Decades had passed since the day Moses stood in front of Egypt's Pharaoh and said, "*This is what the Lord, the God of Israel says, 'Let my people go!'*"[1] Now that must have been a moment to behold! When Charlton Heston[2]-- I mean Moses— spoke these words to Pharaoh, his words should have rendered Pharaoh a quivering mass of human flesh. But did they? No. Listen to what Pharaoh said. "*'Is that so?,' retorted Pharaoh. 'And who is the Lord? Why should I listen to him and let Israel go? I don't know the Lord, and I will not let Israel go.'*"[3]

Oh boy, that did *not* turn out well for Pharaoh.

He was a stubborn man and like most of the world around him, he had reached his viewpoint of reality by observing nature. He and many others had concluded that there were *many* gods . . . and that they required appeasement, not loyalty. Unlike the Israelites, he didn't understand that there is only one God—the Maker of the heavens, the earth and all created things. He had no idea the power of Almighty God. Nor did he know that when God makes a promise, he keeps it!

It took a long time and ten plagues to change his mind. In the meantime, though, life became pretty rough for the people of Israel . . . and they were *none* too happy about it.

Even so, after Pharaoh's stubbornness cost him the life of his own son, he relented and let them go. But then, he changed his mind and chased after them to the edge of the Red Sea. Once again, things didn't turn out very well for him. God parted the Red Sea so that all of his people could walk cross on dry land. But when the Egyptians chased after them again, God let the waters fall back together and destroy them.

I can only imagine what I would have felt if I had been among the Israelites on that day. First of all, seeing the chariots chasing after us, knowing that there is nowhere to go because the Red Sea is in front and the Egyptians are behind us. And then, to see the waters part and to know that God has provided a way of escape! No doubt I would have been more afraid than I had ever been, and yet more relieved than I thought possible! At that point, I would have been the quivering mass of human flesh.

You would think all these incredible events would have caused them to remember and never forget . . . that such things would have made quite the lasting impression.

I must confess that I have been pretty hard on the Israelites as I have read this story over the years. This is probably because I just can't imagine having been rescued from certain death by something as crazy as *the parting of a sea* and then getting all huffy with God a few weeks later when life in the desert gets tough. I've told God more often than I would like to share that if I had been there, and he had done that, I wouldn't have forgotten. Of course, more times than I would like to share, he has reminded me of all the things that he has done on my behalf that seem to fly from my mind the minute my life gets difficult. The truth is that I'm just like them. We all are.

We lose sight of past experiences in the midst of present unpleasantness. It's not really that we have selective memory; it's more that we have selective memory loss. I've learned to refrain from pointing too many fingers at the Israelites because it usually doesn't end well for me.

And as difficult as it may be to imagine, the Israelites' journey towards the land that God had promised them had only just begun when they were delivered from the Egyptians.

Let me give you the condensed version of the story.

They were slaves in Egypt. *God delivered them.* They rejoiced. The Egyptians came after them. They stopped rejoicing. *God parted the Red Sea to save them.* They rejoiced. They went out into the desert and the water tasted funny. They stopped rejoicing. *God provided them sweet water to drink.* They rejoiced. They got hungry. They stopped rejoicing and started complaining. *God sent them manna—food—to eat every day.* They rejoiced. They moved around and finally camped at a place that didn't seem to have enough water. They stopped rejoicing and started demanding. *God directed Moses to strike a rock and pure sparkling water rushed out of it in unending quantities.* They rejoiced. Moses went up onto Mount Sinai to receive the Ten Commandments and they got scared because their leader was gone and stopped rejoicing. They started creating a golden calf to worship instead of God. *God got mad!* Moses interceded on their behalf and called the people to repentance. *God forgave them.* And they rejoiced.[4]

You see where I am going with this? The entire journey from Egypt to the Promised Land was a series of unfortunate events. It didn't seem to matter that God had met their every need . . . that he protected and provided for them. When they were outside the immediate experience of his love and care, they seemed to forget what he had done on their behalf.

By the time they arrived by the Jordan River; forty years had passed, a whole generation had died, and Moses was no longer with them. Their track record was well established and it wasn't great. If God did something good for them, they were going to forget about it soon enough. So this time, God had them approach what he was about to do for them next in a different way, marking the event uniquely and wonderfully.

Picture this. All of Israel is camped on the banks of the Jordan River across from the land God has said he will give to them. They take a good, long look at that river and they don't like what they see. It is a full-sized, raging *river*, not a stream. I can hear them now. *"Joshua, are you serious? How are we going to get to the other side of that? What kind of promised land is it if you can't even get to it?"* Well, that is what I imagine they said . . . it certainly sounds like something I would say under similar circumstances.

But God turned a deaf ear to their murmurings. He told Joshua to instruct the priests to take the Ark of the Covenant—the vessel that contained the tablets of the Ten Commandments, symbolizing God's throne here on earth—and to carry it out into the river and to wait and see what he would do. Joshua sent people throughout the camp to explain what was going to happen the next morning and to tell them to purify themselves because God was going to do great wonders among them.

And they did. The next morning, the priests lifted up the Ark of the Covenant on their shoulders and took a few steps out into the river. And once again, just as the Red Sea had done for their parents' generation, the waters parted. First the women, children and elderly crossed over the riverbed and stepped onto the land on the other side. Then, before the army crossed, God commanded Joshua to have one man from each tribe to go into the river bed directly in front of the place where the priests were standing and to pick up a large stone, place it on their shoulders and carry it to the place where they would camp.

So the twelve men did exactly that. Now, the Bible doesn't tell us anything about this process, but I think we can safely assume that these guys didn't pick up little rocks. I've been around enough guys in these kinds of situations and I can't help but think that there was a bit of healthy competition going on. After all, they had to represent! They were going to show that their tribe was the best tribe. And how could you tell? By the size of the stone each one hefted to their shoulder and managed to carry all the way across, that's how!

Once they were done, Joshua instructed that twelve more stones be piled up in the middle of the riverbed. Then the army crossed over and finally the priests carried the Ark of the Covenant across and onto the shore of the land God had given them. When the last sandaled foot of a priest stepped out of that riverbed, the waters that had been held back were released and filled the dry area again, covering the memorial of stones that had been left there.

The people rejoiced.

And lest they forget again, God had a plan in place to help them remember. He directed them to take those twelve stones and stack them upon each other as a memorial so that in the future when their children asked them about this pile of rocks, they could tell them, *"They remind us that the Jordan River stopped flowing when the Ark of the LORD's Covenant went across. These stones stand as a memorial among the people of Israel forever so that we never forget the faithfulness of the Lord."*[5]

I think of that stack of stones as the twelve *stones of remembrance*. They represented so much. Each stood individually to represent a tribe of Israel. Together, they formed a memorial to help a memory-challenged people to keep the goodness of God and the faithfulness of the Lord alive in their minds forever. These stones also became an intentional talking point for future generations . . . a conversation starter, if you will.

I love that.

You already know that I love the whole process of journaling in my Bible. It has provided me such a wonderful experience in getting to know God better, helping me to remember what I have learned and then giving me an opportunity to respond in a significant and meaningful way to him.

If you have read **Illuminated Journaling** or attended one of my workshops, you know that I talk about the *See and Remember Principle* in Bible Journaling. When we really need to remember something, we ought not rely just on our ability to pluck the memory out of thin air. The *See And Remember Principle* says: if you want to be sure to remember something, leave yourself a *visual reminder*.

Experts who study how the brain works tell us that memory is one of the most perplexing and complicated functions of our cognitive framework. They don't understand exactly how we create a memory, but they do know that it is not all tied up neatly in one place.

I've often joked that I need a better filing system in my head so I can remember things more easily. However, these experts would say that my memory of a single event isn't actually located in one file folder in my brain. In fact, it may actually reside in lots of different file folders—in bits and pieces—until I need the memory. Then, on a good day, my brain goes to work pulling those bits and pieces from their respective locations and putting them back together into a coherent memory. The more we can help our brain find those various folders, the better our memory is going to be. And let's not forget that we have a tendency to have selective memory loss when we don't like our current circumstances— so we need all the help we can get!

Clearly, God knows better than any expert. As our Creator, he knows just how *fearfully and wonderfully made*[6] we truly are. He understands the complexity of our memories and knows precisely how they work—and he certainly can discern the fickleness of our hearts. He is the originator of the *See And Remember Principle.*[7]

Although this was not the first time God had used the *See and Remember Principle* with his people, he purposefully applied it to their arrival into the Promised Land when he had them stack those *stones of remembrance.*

Because I have seen him apply this principle so successfully in our own relationship when I engage with his Word via Bible Journaling, I know that it works to keep what is important in front of my eyes—to help me see and remember what he has taught me. And because I desperately wanted to find a way to have important conversations with my family about the things that matter most in life, I determined to apply what I have learned from the story of the *stones of remembrance* into a different kind of Bible journaling . . . it is what I call *legacy journaling.*

Legacy journaling, while still intensely personal, has an outward focus. It is not so much about discovering new truths in God's Word, although I have learned many wonderful new things while working on my legacy journaling projects. Rather, it is more about intentionally communicating what you have found to be true, whether to future generations in general or to a specific person like a child, grandchild or another important family member. In effect, you are stacking up your own *stones of remembrance.*

I can tell you that while I have used the twelve *stones of remembrance* to form a framework for my legacy journaling, I don't think there is anything particularly sacred about the number twelve in this instance. It was just helpful for me. As I walk you through the choices I have made and dig deeper into the process itself, keep in mind that you may make different choices than me . . . and this is not only okay, but I actually want to encourage you to work through decisions for yourself. One of the things you will find in the **Stones of Remembrance Workbook** is a worksheet for brainstorming your own ideas and then working your way down to your own framework of twelve (or more) stones. This is about documenting God's faithfulness in your life, so feel free to personalize it from the start!

Developing Your Framework

I have a few quirks. One of them I have come to really embrace is that I am a spontaneous girl who also loves to plan. That's quirky, right? I am a bona fide, list making, paper planner toting, box checking, record keeping kind of gal— who doesn't mind going off script when I come up with a harebrained, spontaneously crazy idea. I've reached the conclusion that it is my planner side that allows me to give freedom to the spontaneous side. Rather than fighting with one another, they actually work well together—and I'm grateful that they do because I don't see me giving up either of them anytime soon.

Legacy journaling has been one of those crazy ideas that has benefited from a bit of planning. That old saying, *"If you aim at nothing you will hit it every time,"* isn't very far off the mark. Possessing at least a general framework to guide you will help you to set your sights on where you are headed, while also keeping you from feeling overwhelmed and paralyzed as you begin.

Ask me how I know.

It wasn't long after I finished my first page in my Journaling Bible that I started thinking how cool it would be to create a Bible for my son, Weston, which would be based on my favorite verses and why I loved them. I got a composition book, decorated the cover [of course] and started making a list—several lists, actually.

Then it occurred to me that I should include some of his favorite verses over the course of his life thus far. I turned the page and started a list of those.

Even while I was writing out those lists, I began reflecting on things I had learned from my grandparents that I wished he could benefit from, even though he never met them. I started another page with another list for those things.

And it didn't stop there. I made lists of important events in his life that were evidence of God's love for him personally. I expanded my plan [that's what you do when your idea isn't big enough already] to include his Dad's input . . . Weston and Royce are two points on the opposite ends of the same line and this project wouldn't be complete without whatever Royce wanted to share.

The composition book was beginning to get full, but I wasn't done.

I realized that there were things I wanted him to know about the *character* of God. Next, I pulled out several of my study journals to add a list of the *promises* of God. I considered asking family members to share their life verses for me to work into his Bible. And then. And. And...

Bang—my brain exploded.

I was paralyzed by the sheer magnitude of what I was contemplating. So I did *nothing*.

But I couldn't let go of the idea. As if it weren't bad enough that I really wanted to do this for him and couldn't seem to get started, I began to realize that I wanted to help my sister to do something similar for her kiddos. Over the next year, as I was teaching *Illuminated Journaling Workshops* around the country I kept hearing from participants about how much they wanted to create a Journaling Bible for their kids and grandkids, but they didn't know where to start. And so, like me, they did *nothing*.

The day finally came when my *want to* outgrew my lack of knowing *how to*.

It occurred to me that the frustration I was feeling was familiar. It reminded me of what I felt when I opened my first Journaling Bible. It was fear. Back then my fear was that anything I managed to put on the page wouldn't be good enough. It wasn't an unreasonable fear. What I *wanted* to put on the pages of my Bible exceeded my abilities.

I couldn't draw . . . and this wasn't just my opinion; I had confirmation of that fact. I came across a box of my old report cards while we were cleaning out my Mom's house preparing it for sale. I found it fascinating that even in high school, many of my teachers wrote notes to my parents, most of which were very encouraging letters simply letting my parents know about improvement I had made or areas in which I could do better with more effort. However, one of my freshman report cards contained a note from my art teacher that read: *"Mrs. Saulsberry. It is a good thing you have enrolled your daughter in band as she does not have a creative bone in her body."*

Well that's a fine thing to say! Clearly she didn't live by the old southern adage, *"if you can't say something nice, at least put a **bless her heart** on the end of it!"*

I eventually graduated and moved on with life, but I still carried her words with me and they were being repeated loudly in my head every time I sat down with my Bible to journal in it. These words paralyzed me until my *want to* outgrew my lack of knowing *how to.*

Back then, I asked God to show me how to make beautiful entries in my Bible since he hadn't given me the ability to draw. (Yes, I did say it just about like that. I was a bit perturbed with his apparent stinginess with a gift that I would have found very useful). I should have known that there was an excellent reason he had withheld a natural drawing ability from me: it caused me to find another way to add imagery to my pages—tracing. There isn't a list of rules for Bible Journaling that says: *only those who can draw are allowed to participate*!

If you want to, you ought to! While that isn't a position I subscribe to in most areas of my life, I truly believe that we should aggressively pursue all means available to us to further our relationship with God. No one should be hesitant to approach his throne via his Word just because they believe their skill set isn't quite up to par!

Not only did he help me find a way to accomplish my heart's desire, he also energized me to help other drawing-challenged people do the same by creating my ***Illuminated Journaling*** *Click Prints* and *One and Dones* (line art transfer sheets for tracing images into your Bible.). God's blessings are always multi-faceted. In truth, he had not withheld any good thing from me and he redeemed the pain caused by that long-ago-teacher's thoughtless words. *God is so very good!*

It occurred to me that he might have a similar solution for my current dilemma, if I were to only ask him for direction. This time I was much more polite in my request . . . I do try to learn from my mistakes!

That was when he began to draw my heart back to the passages in Joshua that describe how the *stones of remembrance* came to be. Here are three things that I learned and have begun to apply to my own legacy journaling projects.

Make It Personal

When God told Joshua to have a man from each tribe pick up one stone and carry it to the place where they would camp that night, it was in part so that each tribe would have skin in the game of this memorial. A father could point out to his sons, "That's our stone boys." It was personal to them.

One of the things that had overwhelmed me when I first began working on my legacy journaling project was the fact that I was attempting to point out *all* the worthy things in God's Word. It sounds kind of silly when I say it that way, right? Weston already has access to the whole of God's Word, so what I needed to do in this gift was to share what is *personal* to me about it. In a way, a legacy journal is a personal testimony of the faithfulness of God in the lives of an individual or a family.

When I meet someone who doesn't know Jesus yet, I rarely start by quoting scripture to them. I almost always begin by telling them what Jesus has meant to me in my own day-to-day living. Whether someone is asking you for a recommendation to a restaurant or how to know Jesus better, they are asking for your personal experience. *What has worked for you? What do you wish someone had told you before you had to discover it on your own?*

Like the old family Bibles our new ones are living documentation of the major events in our lives. You will probably want to record some births, marriages and deaths. Those things are evidence of God's faithfulness in your personal family. I have begun giving new mothers and brides a Journaling Bible with just one entry in it . . . something personal to them.

For expectant moms, I love to grab photos with their "baby bumps" that they have posted to their own Facebook pages. For each mom, I print out their photo and trace it into the Bible I  am going to give her—like you see here in this picture. I used Psalm 71:6, *"Upon you I have leaned from before my birth; You are he who took me from my mother's womb and my praise is continually of you."* It is very personal. (A full color version of this art is available on the pages after Chapter 4).

One of the most important personal stories you can share is your actual testimony. How did you come to know Christ? Where did it happen? What was your life like before and after you entered into that personal relationship with him? If you are doing this Bible for one of your kiddos, add their story as well . . . we all love to read about ourselves!

When Weston was in second grade, he was just too busy being a boy to want to do much reading. But in the evenings, he would sometimes wind down just enough to come sit on the couch and let me read to him while I rubbed his feet.

[Don't judge me . . . I wasn't above a little bribery to sweeten the deal!] When we first started doing it, he would tell me that the stories just weren't interesting. Finally, I had a brainstorm and told him I had found a book about boy named Weston who was a bit of a sleuth. That piqued his interest. Fortunately, there were dozens of books about "Weston" available. Oh yes, most people know them because they have read about a boy named *Encyclopedia Brown*, but in our version, the boy's name was always Weston. Sometimes a mom has to do what a mom has to do! I've used this same idea in my Legacy Journaling projects. It is great to personalize a promise with the actual name of the person you are doing it for.

For Jeremiah 29:11 I love to fill the whole margin with the verse personalized with their name. *"For I know the plans I have for Weston. They are plans for his good and not for disaster. Plans to give him a future and a hope."* That may be all that you want to do. It is enough to bring that verse into their view so it will be there when they need to remember that God has good plans for them—that they have good reason to place their hope in him. If there is more that needs to be said, just pop over to the other margin and write them a note.

Our relationship with Jesus is so very personal . . . let your Legacy Journaling reflect that.

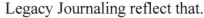

Let A Few Stand For the Whole

I'm afraid that if I had been in charge of creating the *stones of remembrance* memorial that it would have really gotten out of hand. My event planner brain has a switch that says, *"If one is good, two are better,"* and *"More makes it memorable."* That might work for party planning, but I'm glad that God didn't command every single person to pick up a rock on their trek across the riverbed. That would have taken foreeeverrrrrrrr—particularly if even one of those children had my love of rocks!

My Mom was a smarty. Every vacation, she would make a big deal about all of us finding the perfect rock to bring back as our souvenir. Oh yes, I see your head nodding. Brilliant, right? It was an activity that could hold a child's attention for quite some time and it established that sometimes the most valuable souvenir was also the *free* one. Feel free to use that one yourself if you hadn't already thought of it.

I always loved the process of finding the perfect stone. I would pick one up and walk around with it until I found one I liked better. To this day, I always have a rock or two in my suitcase to bring back from a trip to a new place. Asking me to pick a rock on my way across the riverbed into the Promised Land would have been a disaster.

It wasn't just to save on time that God allowed a few to stand for the whole. Can you imagine how big the memorial would have to be to include even a small pebble from each person? According to a census taken in Numbers 26, there were more than 600,000 able-bodied men in their camp. And this count did not take into account the women, children, or elderly men. Whoa! Sometimes less really is more.

This is why I decided to choose twelve topics or themes upon which to focus my Legacy Journaling, in addition to all of the personal entries we just discussed. I will be sharing more about that process in the upcoming chapters, but I want to offer my rationale for limiting them to just the twelve. You may choose more—or less. I found that I was less overwhelmed with a more finite set of themes to focus upon . . . and when I stopped being overwhelmed, I actually started journaling.

Make It Do-able In The Midst Of Real Life

God's plan for the memorial was one that the people of Israel could accomplish *while* they were also doing the very important task of migrating as many as a million people from one side of a river to the other. My days are already chock-full of really important things to accomplish—and so are yours. This process has to be doable in the midst of real life.

We will discover many of the things I have done to keep this project manageable, but there are three basic ideas that changed my approach and have remained my foundation for doing Legacy Journaling in the midst of my real life.

The first is being intentional about setting aside time to work on it. I gave up one of my favorite weekly TV shows to have more time to work on it and I haven't regretted one minute of it. Now before you think I'm all that and a bag of chips because I made this particular choice, know that I binge watch my favorite show on *Hulu* when I am traveling and staying in a hotel. It takes much less time to watch a show that way and it is a great way to wind down after a long day. [Yeah, I know that was a total rationalization . . . I'll give that one to you.].

The second is to keep a small collection of supplies where they are easily accessible when you have a few minutes to work. You will see that I fall back on my favorite techniques for the vast majority of my journaling—so I have a basket that I keep filled with watercolors, colored pencils, tracing supplies, a stack of pre-cut watercolor paper, washi tape, a couple of paint brushes, a few pens and a pencil. I can grab them and take them with me to a night of journaling with my friends or into the family room to be with my family when we are all home for an evening. The key is that I have supplies already available when I find myself with time to work.

Finally, try to avoid being super focused on it when you aren't working on it. I do think about it quite a bit while I am doing other things, but I don't beat myself up because I *ought* to be working on it when I find a few minutes. I let my mind think of ideas and I jot them down in my planner. You will find examples of what I use in the ***Stones of Remembrance Workbook***. I almost always have my planner with me so I can make a few notes and then pull them out when I sit down to actually work on it.

These three things helped me move from being paralyzed to being energized . . . and I hope that is what you are beginning to feel as well!

Notes

[1] Exodus 5:1 New Living Translation, Tyndale House Publishing.
[2] Charlton Heston played Moses in the 1956 release of the movie,
The Ten Commandments directed by Cecil B. DeMille.
[3] Exodus 5:2 New Living Translation, Tyndale House Publishing.
[4] Exodus 5:1 – 40:38 New Living Translation, Tyndale House Publishing.
[5] Joshua 4 New Living Translation, Tyndale House Publishing.
[6] Psalm 139:13-15 English Standard Version, Crossway Books
[7] *Illuminated Journaling*, Jann Gray, pp. 20-21.

CHAPTER 2

Standing On The Unshakeable Rock

L ife changes so quickly. One moment, we are standing on solid ground and the next, we find ourselves knee deep in quicksand.

Even as I write these words, I am sitting here with tears still wet upon my face.

A dear friend sent me a message this morning asking for prayer for a family who has just lost their son. I don't know them personally, but as I prayed for God to comfort them, my mother's heart wept with them. As parents, we are not meant to outlive our children. From the moment they come to us, we spend our lives preparing them to live full lives even when we will no longer be here to guide them. This means we spend our whole lives believing we will be the first ones to go . . . not them.

Pain this deep turns the world, as we know it, upside down. It shakes our equilibrium.

Right seems wrong.

Up seems down.

We can't trust our senses because they will lie to us. Like pilots using instruments to fly in zero visibility conditions, we have to use what we know will never lie to us—the goodness of God. He isn't just good sometimes. He is good even in the midst of the very worst situation. His Word—his love letter to us so we can know His heart—tells us:

He will never leave us or forsake us.[1]

His plans for us are good...plans that are filled with hope and a future.[2]

Pain fills our heart and clouds our eyes, so when we can't see God's hands or understand the "why" of our situation, we have to trust His heart.

Days like these are why I am so passionate about helping us dig down deep into God's Word so we can move as much of it as possible from our heads to our hearts. There will be days that we *have to know* that *we know that we know* we can trust the *goodness* of God.

That he is:

Powerful,
Mighty,
Merciful,
Loving,
Tender,
Fierce,
Jealous,
Just,

Wise,
Majestic
and *Kind.*[3]

We just have to know it with every fiber of our being!

The time to try and build up your strength isn't at the start of a marathon—it's in the training you do before the gun goes off. Oh don't get me wrong, if you are mid-race thinking you were running a 5K only to find that you are actually in mile two of a marathon, there is no better place to go than to the feet of Jesus and His Word. But I know from personal experience that having His Word and the truth that it contains lodged down deep in my heart makes it easier to draw upon in times of sadness, disappointment and confusion.

You may have wondered why I asked Josh McDowell to write the foreword of this book. No, it isn't because he does Bible journaling—although I know for a fact that the margins of his Bible are filled with personal notes. It is because my encounters as a thirteen year old with him and his wife, Dottie, changed how I view scripture. Josh is a leading authority on the reliability of scripture and when you babysit for his kids, you end up getting more out of the experience than a little bit of spending money!

Their oldest, Kelly, was just two years old when I began babysitting for them. The second time I stayed with Kelly, Josh gave me an assignment. I guess he thought that a two year old was going to go to bed long before they got home. He either thought I was really good or he didn't yet know much about two-year olds! The assignment was to read a chapter out of his book, *Evidence That Demands A Verdict.*[4] Have you seen that book? It's a seriously large book to read! But I am so glad that I did.

I loved staying with Kelly, and later Sean, but I grew to love the time in between when they went to bed and when Josh and Dottie arrived home from their dates. I had always loved God's Word, but I had never even thought to ask, *"Is it reliable? Or can it be trusted?"*

The answers to those questions are the foundation for whether we believe that God is who he says he is and can do what he says he can do. If I am going to rely on him, I have to trust him and that starts with trusting his Word.

Each time, I would pour over the chapter that had been assigned to me and it wasn't long before I had questions. I finally found a use for the legal pad and pencil that Josh always left beside the book. Smart man. Now that I think of it, it might have been Dottie who showed such forethought. My most vivid memories of that summer are when Josh would walk me home. They lived at one end of the block and my family lived in the second house from the other end. He would pick up the legal pad and we would head out. He would ask me which of the questions I had written down confused me the most and we would start there. We would walk and talk . . not with him doing all the talking and me doing all the listening. It was a dialogue. And if we made it to my end of the block and my question wasn't totally answered, we would just circle around the block again.

That experience is why I became a missionary. I believed that everybody needed somebody who was willing to go around the block again until it was clear why they needed a Savior.

I learned so much that summer—and what I learned gave me confidence that God's Word was reliable, accurate and could be trusted.

It is a different subject than this book was designed to deal with, but if you have not yet found the answers to these questions for yourself, I want to encourage you to do so. Getting them answered isn't an academic exercise; it is about your heart. You will fall in love with Jesus and his Word all over again and you will be more certain than ever that he is worthy of your love and devotion.

I love how Beth Moore puts it: *"Following Jesus is meant to be driven and drawn by love. Audacious love."* [5]

She is so right. Love compels us! I have wanted that for myself in my relationship with Jesus and that is why I have come to love *Illuminated Journaling* so very much. The very process moves me past merely reading scriptures to seeing them come alive to the point that they capture my heart and compel me to take the time to respond to them on the pages of my Bible. It is a process that made sense to me when I began thinking about a *Legacy Journaling* project as well.

You may already be familiar with *Illuminated Journaling* or Bible Journaling, but I don't want to assume that just because you've picked up this particular book, you have already been using this process for your own study and reflection. But even if you have been journaling for a while, I want to share a few elements of *Illuminated Journaling* that I have found to be extremely relevant to the choices I made when starting my own *Legacy Journaling* projects.

But before we jump into that, I need to address the elephant in the room. If you are new to *Illuminated Journaling*, you may have thought I couldn't see him—big ears, trunk and all. I can... and in fact, me and the elephant are old friends. He just doesn't bother me much anymore. So let's deal with the question that is meandering around in the back of your mind, if not on the tip of your tongue.

"Are you actually writing and drawing on the pages of your Bible?"

Yes, *Illuminated Journaling* encourages you to write, draw, doodle, sketch, paint and stamp right onto the pages of your Bible. I know that the thought of doing that might make you just a bit uncomfortable—or maybe *a lot* uncomfortable. In my enthusiasm to introduce you to joys of journaling in your Bible, I do not want to ignore what might be your biggest inhibition about it.

So let me be clear. I *love* the Word of God! I approach it with reverence and awe. I do not want to treat it lightly or with *any* disrespect. What I feel is okay for me may not feel right for everyone. I do not think that I occupy the only "enlightened" position here.

I remember how I felt as I removed the wrapping and opened the cover on my first Journaling Bible. I was struck by how clean and pristine the pages were—and for the first time I acknowledged the unspoken question that had been lurking in the back of my mind. *"God, if I start journaling in my Bible, are You going to consider this an act of irreverence—a defacing of Your Word? Or will You see what I am doing as my way of wanting to get to know You better and offer You a gift of praise with my heART?"*

I think everyone who wants to begin *Illuminated* or *Legacy Journaling* needs to have this conversation with God, asking Him these questions personally. I hold God's Word in *reverence* because it is His personal message to you and me—how we get to know Him. I want to treat it respectfully. But I have also come to realize that the book that holds the *words* of God is much like the church building housing the *people* of God. Both should be taken care of and treated with respect, but we should never consider them holier than the actual words or people contained within.

Church looks different depending on the people who attend. Some churches are formal, while others are more casual. Some use hymnals, while others sing worship songs from lyrics projected onto a screen. They may look very different, but underneath they serve the same purposes: *to reach people for Christ, disciple them in their faith and send the people of the church out into the world to be ambassadors for Christ.*

Anything that does not detract from those *purpose*s is simply *preference.*

I am blessed to own several Bibles. They too look different. I have some that I love to use for studying because they provide me with invaluable word study resources. Others seem better suited for reading for comprehension—they use words that are easier for me to understand and look more like a chapter in a book without verse numbers. I have one Bible version that I take to church with me because my pastor uses a version that I do not regularly use, and I like being able to read along with him and not be distracted by the fact that my favorite Bible says it a little bit differently. They look different, but they all serve the same purpose—*to reveal God and His character to me, showing me how to live a holy and righteous life and making clear my need for a Savior within God's plan for my salvation.* Again, anything that does not detract from that purpose is *preference.*

I have found that journaling *in* my Bible helps reveal the Word of God as the living, breathing voice *inside* my heart that it truly is. That is exactly what God wants His Word to do in my life, so my journaling is fulfilling the purpose of His Word. I'm not slopping paint on the page just to create art—I am approaching His Word reverently and recording what I have learned when I have met with Him in the pages of my Bible. I have very intentionally asked Him to reveal to me if He has *any* displeasure with what I am doing. I have not experienced a single check in my spirit. However, I do continue to occasionally bring the subject up again and ask Him to be the Guide of my work in my Bible. I can honestly say that when I am working in my Bible, I feel His pleasure.

I think we should each ask the Lord how He feels about it. Does He feel that the time that you spend journaling in the Word is helping your relationship? Does He see it as an act of worship? Or does He feel that you are defacing His Word? Ask and then listen. Not with a heart that thinks it knows the answers because of how we have "always" approached His Word, but rather with a heart seeking to know if we have His approval to approach His Word in this manner.

I especially want to encourage you to have these conversations if you are not already a personal journaler. Having talked with God about it before you open a Bible to begin a legacy project will help you avoid having that silly elephant show up in your room unexpectedly. He's a stubborn, old, peanut-loving, large-footprint-leaving soul and he just won't go away until you shoo him out properly!

If you have felt that you have God's permission to proceed, then using some of the things we have learned from our personal journaling will help you be successful when you begin creating a legacy project.

The See And Remember Principle

We talked about one aspect of the *See and Remember Principle* in Chapter One—that if you want to remember something, *create a visual reminder for yourself.* But the principle is deeper than just providing us with a quick memory tool. The use of imagery in our journaling is a compelling element all its own.

When I add imagery to my Bible, there are times when the creative process can be even more satisfying than writing notes in the margin. Sometimes the imagery seems to find a way to communicate more accurately what I am feeling about God and what I want to remember—and it does so in such a way that words alone could never do.

Images have the ability to transport us back to a moment in time and remind us of the details of that moment as if they happened yesterday. Images bring the past into the present. They bring a spiritual lesson to the forefront of our memory, refreshing our minds and hearts.

Something really remarkable happens when we engage in using imagery with our time in the Word. When we take the time to express what we have learned in a tangible way—with words and images—it is like the flash of the camera casting illumination on the subject and recording that particular moment in time in a way that ensures our ability to return to this truth time and again. We don't have to re-learn the truth; we can recall it and if need be, recommit to making it part of our daily walk.

Using imagery in our legacy projects taps into all the same reasons we use it in our personal journaling as well. We are counting on the effort we put into creating these very special Bibles to have an impact on the viewer. Using imagery will not only help them remember what you share with them but it also has the power to move them ahead into learning it for themselves, perhaps for the first time.

Adding imagery onto a Bible page can be a bit intimidating . . . I *know*! But because it adds such a powerful element to the page, I try to move past the intimidation factor and do it anyway. Remember, imagery isn't just a drawing [or a tracing, in my case]. It could be a stamped image that you have colored in, text that you have rewritten to draw attention to the key phrases or even die cuts and stickers as well. The key is to figure out what works best for the concept you are seeking to illustrate.

To help me in that process, I do a few things.

Give Yourself Time To Think

I rarely begin working on an entry immediately after I have completed a study or determined the topic I want to cover in my *Legacy Journaling Bible*. There are certainly exceptions to this pattern, but for the most part, to begin immediately would feel like I was forcing myself to describe an experience that I had not yet fully savored. I'm not very knowledgeable about winemaking, but I remember an old commercial on television with the tagline: *"We will sell no wine before its time!"* I always thought it was a brilliant commercial because it communicated to the consumer that the quality of their experience was worth the time it took to make it right. That is how I feel about the responsive process of *Illuminated* and *Legacy Journaling*.

Rarely is my first thought my best thought. My goal is not to figure out how to create a journaling page in my Bible as quickly as possible. I prefer to linger—to tarry and see what other ideas may occur to me.

Most of the time, this process takes place over a few hours, or even a few days. I think about it when I am driving, cooking or grocery shopping [just another reason to bring a list with you.] I talk to God about it during my prayer times. During these times, I begin to "try on" ideas of imagery that I may want to use when I journal about it.

It is a lot like going into the dressing room with a stack of dresses to try on. You've kind of pre-selected a few options before you enter, but once it is just you and that poorly lit room with the wavy mirror, your decision-making begins in earnest. Because, while all of the dresses are nice, they may not be perfect for you and that is *exactly* the reason why you must try them on before you decide.

Identify the Heartbeat

I seek to identify exactly what about this study (if it is for personal journaling) or topic (for legacy journaling) grabbed my heart and mind so much that I feel compelled to do an entry about it. The answer isn't always a new thought or idea, but it is the one that if someone were to say it out loud in your hearing, your heart would want to respond with an affirming, *"Mmmm hmmmm, that's right!"* Your head might even start nodding involuntarily. It simply resonates with you.

It's the heartbeat that makes the idea have a life of it's own.

Hebrews describes the Word of God this way. *"For the word of God is living and active, sharper than any two-edged sword, piercing to the division of soul and of spirit, of joints and of marrow, and discerning the thoughts and intentions of the heart."* If I try on an illustration and it seems to dull the edge of the sword, I know I haven't found the right one yet.

One cautionary suggestion: *don't throw out a perfectly good idea because you don't think you could draw it.* Mmmm hmmm . . . ask me how I know you need to avoid that pitfall! We are going to talk more about this later and you will find many more tips and tricks to assist you in adding illustrations to your project in the ***Stones of Remembrance Workbook***, but the key to remember is this: even if you don't feel that you can draw, try on several ideas and stick with the one that looks best on *you.*

Your journaling will always benefit from giving it time. As you identify the *stones of remembrance* that you want to focus on in your project, give yourself time to think about which scriptures best express what you want to say. Think about if this topic just needs an entry that highlights the words, or would an illustration or personal letter of testimony in the margin accomplish your purposes best? Each one will be different.

Allow Your Creative Self To Be Revealed

In addition to being unkind, my high school art teacher was wrong! We are all born with a creative bone in our body—I have one and so do you because we are both made in the image of our Creator. That doesn't mean that you automatically have a natural ability to draw. I certainly don't. I also don't have a natural ability to play the piano, but after many years of lessons in my childhood, I can still sit down and play for my own enjoyment . . . and I don't regret a single moment spent learning the *skills* necessary to be able to do so.

Creativity is something you have because God placed it within you. Drawing, painting, writing, playing the piano, making a quilt, or writing a song or a poem are all expressions of that creativity. They are also skills—and skills can be learned.

I had to set aside the desire for my creations to perfect and excellent before I thought they would be worthy enough to be added to the pages of my Bible.

As I say in my workshops all the time; *"Journaling is more about your **heart** than the art!"* I can't stress that enough. I can teach you to do the art—you just start with your heart and let the creativity flow from there. The entries you create out of the fullness of your heart are the kinds of entries you want to leave behind. Do I still wish that everything I created would be museum-worthy, or at least wall-worthy? Sure I do—but everything isn't and that is okay. I certainly don't let it stop me from creating, particularly when we are talking about personal *Illuminated Journaling.* You are creating for an audience of One! He has already called you worthy and will take delight in your offering. You need to take whatever you create to your Father with the spirit of a five year old who knows that it is refrigerator-worthy! He will gladly receive it and find a place on his refrigerator for it.

Of course, people who walk the earth among us are not always so kind, nor do they have special lenses in their glasses that help them see our intent and our heart. And goodness knows, they don't all have a filter over their mouths to keep them from speaking unkind words without so much as a thought or a "bless your heart!" But let's not let a little thing like that stop us.

Let's be ***braveful***. In case you are wondering, that is a word I made up. It's a useful ability—making up words when no other words quite work. I think this situation calls for a word such as *braveful!*

To be *braveful* means to not only fill ourselves with as much bravery as we can muster, but to ask God to give us the extra measure we need to be adequate to the task. It isn't the same as being fearless. I am still fearful when I sit down to journal. I don't know that it is going to turn out as I want or expect—and there is a real chance it will not. But besides our universe, I don't think anything great has ever been created in the absence of fear. If you are absolutely certain of something, where is the greatness in it? It is when we invite God to be part of the process that we can move past our fear and be *braveful!*

When you sit down to work on an entry in a *Legacy Journaling* project, you've expanded your audience beyond just your Heavenly Father. There will be other eyes on it. Don't let the fear of that audience rob you of expressing what is really in your heart. You will communicate your heart the best when you free it from the fear of not being understood or well-received, trusting God to help you do your best.

And to help you to do your best, you may want to practice. Increase your skills. Use aids like **One and Dones**™, **Click Prints**™ or stamps and stickers. But don't let a little thing like not believing you are a natural artist stop you. Be *braveful*. Do it anyway! You didn't take on this project to showcase your ability; you did it to showcase God and his legacy of faithfulness in your life. I'll help you with the other stuff.

Legacy Journaling Will Encourage Them To Try It For Themselves

In my heart of hearts, I don't want whatever my final entry is in one of these Bible to be the last thing that is ever added to it. I want my Bible to be a place where whoever has possession of it feels that they can continue adding to it their own thoughts and experiences. I don't want it to be tucked away like a completed work—I desire for my entries to be a starting point only. When *Legacy Journaling* gives way to personal *Illuminated Journaling* it means that the Word has compelled them to actively participate . . . and I can't imagine a more exciting thing to happen to one of these projects!

They may never even know that *Illuminated Journaling* was even a *thing*, but if they are intrigued by what they see, I will have modeled for them how it is done and then they too can benefit from the process for themselves. Their style doesn't need to match mine . . . the Bible is a place to document the stories of our common love for Jesus. Their story will look different than mine, so our art and the entries we create should reflect as much.

After you give your *Legacy Journaling* Bible to a loved one, wouldn't you be delighted to discover that they have begun an *Illuminated Journaling* adventure of their own simply because your gift provided them the invitation to do so?

I created a journaling Bible for a young bride a couple of years ago as a gift. I added a picture of her and her husband's first home together near the verse *"as for me and my house, we will serve the Lord."* [6] Her mother is a dear friend of mine and has sent me a couple of pictures of additional pages her daughter has added to her Bible. It thrills my heart to see how she has taken my gift and made it her own. To me, that is what *Legacy Journaling* is all about.

Our whole reason for starting a project like this is to encourage the people we love to dig down deep into God's Word and move as much of it as possible from their heads to their hearts. Their lives will be filled with ups and downs. The ground under them will sometimes quake, shaking them to their core. They will need to know that they know *they know* they can stand on the unshakeable rock of God and His Word. Your gift just may be the impetus they need to begin hiding God's Word in their hearts for themselves!

Let it be so, Lord, let it be so!

Notes

[1] Deuteronomy 31:8

[2] Jeremiah 29:11

[3] Powerful - Psalm 29:4; Mighty - Psalm 50; Merciful - Luke 6:36; Loving - 1 Peter 5:7; Tender - Luke 1:78; Fierce - Deuteronomy `3:17; Jealous - Exodus 20:5; Just - Deuteronomy 32:4; Wise – Roman 16:27; Majestic – Psalm 29:4; Kind – Titus 3:4

[4] *The New Evidence That Demands a Verdict,* Josh McDowell, Thomas Nelson, 1999 For an easier read but equally informative, I highly recommend *God Breathed* by Josh McDowell, Barbour Publishing, 2015.

[5] Beth Moore, *Audacious*, Lifeway Christian Publishers, 2016, p 25.

[6] Joshua 24:15

CHAPTER 3

Foundation Stones

Every summer I spent a couple of weeks with my grandparents. I began looking forward to my next two-week vacation with them the moment I came home from the last one. My time with them offered a change from the regular rhythms of my days of school, my studies and my extracurricular activities as well. It was unfettered access to two of the people I loved the most. The reason I so highly anticipated those visits wasn't that we always did super amazing things . . . it was that my grandparents welcomed me into the midst of their lives and managed to turn the ordinary happenings of a day into extraordinary adventures.

Jammy Jane took in ironing to help make ends meet. As soon as Gramps left for the day, she would pull out her ironing board, along with a basket of mostly white shirts. She would iron, and we would talk—her hands never still, always keeping her iron in motion. She would lift it occasionally when she was working on a particularly stubborn shirt to dip her hand in a bowl of water and shake it to distribute the drops of water over the material . . . just to help get the last of the wrinkles out. Once she was satisfied with the result, she would follow up with a quick spritz of bottled starch to add crispness to those once limp, white shirts.

To this day, the smell of starched shirts takes me back to those summer days and brings a smile to my face.

It wasn't long before I asked if I could help. At once,, Jammy Jane retrieved an old ironing board from the closet, along with another iron and my own bowl of water. Even after she had adjusted the board's height as low as it would go, I still wasn't tall enough. But Jammy Jane never gave up easily, so she found some old phone books for me to stand on, wrapping them in a towel to make them steadier. Once she was satisfied with the setup, she showed me how to place a shirt on the board and use the curved portion of it to get into tight places. She taught me to not press on the iron, but to let the heat and the motion do the work. She demonstrated the flicking motion that would distribute the best drops of water from my hand. And then she went back to her own board and let me learn by doing.

Jammy Jane was a wise woman . . . and I learned more than just about ironing that day.

I learned:

Work isn't work when you are having fun.

A job takes less time when more hands are applied to it.

Give a new "ironer" a shirt that doesn't matter. [Gramps proudly wore the shirt I ironed for him the next day . . . iron print and all.]

Use simple tools when simple tools will work.

Use better tools if you have access to them.

Simply put, some jobs are best accomplished with simple tools—like a bowl of water or a padded ironing board. But there are other times when better tools will produce better results. After I became a bit more proficient with my iron, Jammy Jane let me come over and try hers out. Oh. My. Stars. Her iron was twice the weight of mine. It took some getting used to, but the added weight made such a difference in how quickly I could finish a shirt. To this day, I opt for a heavier iron because if you have to iron, you might as well get it done as quickly as you can . . . especially if you don't have anyone to talk to!

The same is true when it comes to picking out your tools and supplies to use in your Legacy Journaling Bible. You can accomplish a lot with very simple and inexpensive products. There are, however, a couple of places where I suggest you spend a little more money (if you can) because you will be more satisfied with the results. I will point those out as we go along.

Begin by picking out the Bible you will use. There are so many good wide margin journaling Bibles available now and you can most likely find one that is published in your favorite Bible version. Check several of them out—and you also may want to determine if the person for whom you are creating this Legacy Journaling Bible has a certain version preference.

While I have seen some people use a Bible that belonged to someone in their family to create their Legacy Journaling project [and it was really cool,] as a general rule, I don't recommend using an heirloom Bible for a several reasons. The first is that it will just add more pressure upon you that this project doesn't need. The fear of messing up on the pages of an heirloom Bible will make it difficult for you to create freely. It will remove some of the joy of working on it. Secondly, since you will be adding content onto these pages, using a Bible that is older might mean that the pages are more fragile than you anticipate and won't hold up. And finally, trust me when I say that you will really come to love the wide-open spaces found in the margins of today's journaling Bibles. Most margins are at least two inches wide and give you ample space in which to create and write. Finding this much space in an heirloom Bible would be a challenge.

Regardless of which Bible you choose to use, you need to keep in mind that the paper used in Bible printing is generally quite different from any other kind of art paper you may have ever used before. It will be thinner. It may be coated. The publisher selected the paper in your Bible because it can stand up to a lot of handling, not because it works well with paint and inks. So you will need to test any supplies you plan to use, even if you have seen someone else use them with beautiful results. There is so much variance between the paper found in different Bibles, as well as in the way a journaler uses a certain product, that you do not want to assume you will see the same results.

This is where having a personal *Illuminated Journaling* Bible can really come in handy. I actually laughed as I typed that last sentence. You should have seen that one coming! Of course I am a proponent of having your own Bible in which to journal—and being able to practice in it is the least of all the reasons to encourage you to do so . . . but it's still a good one! I have dedicated the last few pages in my Bible as a "test kitchen" of sorts. I cannot stress enough that one of the best ways to be happy with your results is to be very familiar with what a certain product does on the page of your Bible. If you already are a journaler, consider finding a Bible printed by the same publisher for your Legacy Journaling Bible. You will already be familiar with the paper and how it interacts with all of your favorite mediums. This will lend you a sense of freedom as you create each of your entries.

Basic Tools and Supplies

You don't need to make a huge investment to start journaling. However, I do recommend gathering a few basic supplies including:

Mechanical Pencil (.07 or.05)
White Eraser
Permanent Black Ink Pens in a variety of nib sizes
White Gel Pen
Watercolor Palette
Colored Pencils
Gamsol/Odorless Mineral Spirits
Blending Stumps/Qtips
Tracing Paper
Graphite Paper
Roll of Washi tape
Metal Ball Stylus

If you are a beginner, I recommend starting with mid-quality, student grade products. These are typically less expensive and you can still achieve great results with them.

It will be helpful to offer a little more detail on each of these items to help you if who are just getting started. They may seem a little self-explanatory, but I am hoping that by giving you just a bit of context, you will benefit from the fact that I have learned it the *hard way*!

Mechanical Pencil and White Eraser

These two tools will become your best friends. You may be wondering why I have been so specific about them when we all have a good old #2 pencil hanging around the house somewhere. The reason is that unless you are doing a pencil sketch as your artwork, you will ultimately want to erase your pencil lines and the smaller they are, the less you have to erase. A #2 pencil will dull very quickly, thus leaving fatter and fatter marks. But a mechanical pencil stays sharp and fine from the first to the last mark you leave on the page.

A white latex eraser is the best for erasing both mechanical pencil and colored pencils. Red rubber erasers seem to grab the page and mar it with wrinkles and red marks that are almost impossible to remove.

Permanent Black Ink Pens

I use Microns™ by Sakura in nibs 1, 05, 03 and 005 (the larger the number, the wider the nib). I've tried a lot of different pens, and while everyone has their favorites. I have settled on Microns™ as my personal choice for a couple of reasons. Most importantly, they do not bleed through untreated, prepped Bible paper. They are also permanent, meaning they do not react to water. I so often use watercolor in my journaling that I need to use a pen so I can paint right over and not be afraid that it is going to reactivate, making a mess of my page. Microns™ are economical, come in a wide variety of nibs and ink colors and seem to work well with the widest variety of other paints and inks that I have used for Bible journaling.

I will give you two cautionary notes about working with them that probably are true of other permanent ink pens as well. First, particularly with the wider nibs, you will need to give the ink a few seconds to dry before adding anything to it. Because the ink doesn't seep down into the page and bleed through, it means that it is actually floating on top of it until it is dry. When you use a larger nib, you are depositing a larger amount of ink onto the page and should allow a bit of extra time to let it dry. Secondly, these pens will write on a wide variety of paint, pencils and ink, but you need to make sure that whatever you are writing on top of is totally dry before reaching for your pen. The nibs on these pens are particularly susceptible to getting clogged by wet paint and once they are clogged, just say goodbye and move on to another pen. I'm an impatient journaler and I always want to move on to the next stage as quickly as possible—but do yourself and your pens a favor: let wet paint *totally* dry before you reach for your permanent pens.

There are many other types of pens and ink that you can use if you decide that you want to prepare your pages with a product that seals the page and keeps ink or paint from seeping through. I will be talking about that a little later in the chapter, but I wanted to again emphasize that one of the reasons that I personally use Micron™ pens is I don't have to take the extra step of prepping my page before I start working on it . . . *if* I am going to solely work with the basic products I have just shared.

White Gel Pen

I use the Classic Gel pen by Sakura because it will literally write on just about anything and it keeps a nice, crisp white color on top of watercolors and other dye inks. Adding a few highlights and details to an illustration or text treatment is what gives it a finishing touch. A simple white gel pen can do that beautifully.

With the advent of the popularity of coloring books, there are a host of gel pens on the market. They seem to work very well on the paper being used in the coloring books and they come in a wonderful variety of bright colors. I've tried a lot of them and I have found that many of these gel pens do not perform well when used directly on Bible paper. For some reason, and, they bleed right through. If you already have some gel pens in your craft stash, please test them first to make sure you will not be disappointed with the results.

The Classic Gel pen by Sakura comes in a variety of colors as well. I particularly like to use their Gold, Silver and Copper gel pens for touches of metallic goodness on my pages.

Watercolor Palette

I think I may have just heard you gasp. I know it seems like it would be the *worst* thing to use, but Bible pages actually seem to like it. I use watercolor all the time in my journaling and I almost never prep my page ahead of time. Bible paper is created with a bit of a chemical in it called *sizing*. It is put into the paper to make it resist the oil and dirt that comes from frequent handling of the pages. Regular books don't have this sizing in them because they just don't have to hold up to the wear that Bible pages do when we return over and over to the same page. The sizing is what makes a Bible page feel a little slick. And, if you know a couple of tricks, sizing is what makes working with watercolors a wonderful experience.

I rarely start a page without using watercolors. Watercolor is a wonderful transparent medium that you can read right through, so you don't have to worry about covering up words on the page. Even if I am only going to write a letter or a prayer in the margin, I can create a quick background for a page with a couple of shades of watercolor and a few splatters with coordinating colors. It just grounds the whole page, giving it a lovely backdrop upon which to set.

For pages I intend to illustrate, I use watercolors to *color block* in the image after tracing it onto the page. I can then quickly add shading and detail with colored pencils after establishing the basic colors with watercolor.

Yes, using watercolors will make your pages crinkle just a bit. But you can counteract that in a couple of ways. First, if you use a craft heat tool or a hairdryer to dry the page as you are working on it (and I highly recommend that you do), you can tug at the edge of the page to encourage the page to flatten out. Also, when you are finished with the page and it is totally dry, shut the Bible and place a couple of heavy books on top of it like you are pressing flowers between its pages. I don't recommend ironing your pages because if you have used colored pencils on any page in your Bible, the heat from the iron will melt the wax and cause a mess. *Ask me how I know!* Your page will be *flat-er*, but it will still change the texture of the page just a bit. I actually have come to love the feel of paper that has been painted on. As I am turning the pages, it is like my fingers know before my eyes do that I am about to come to a page on which I have already spent time. *Bonus!*

Here are a few things to get you started with watercolors. When working with watercolors, you need to think about them a little differently than you would if you were working on watercolor paper. Our goal is to use them while they float on the top of the page, so you will want to avoid scrubbing the page with your paintbrush because that will break down the sizing and cause them to seep through. For that reason, I encourage you to use more water than you think you need. If you are working with a dry brush, you are more likely to scrub at the page to try and make your paint go further—so a wet brush will actually do better than a dry brush. I tell my students that if it isn't shiny when you put it on the page, it probably isn't wet enough. Practice making watery watercolor washes on your test pages in the **Stones of Remembrance Workbook**.

Another trick to getting great results with watercolors is to work in layers. Keep a craft heat tool or a hair dryer near by and *dry your page often*. Start with a light wash of color and then dry it. You can always add to it and you will quickly get to the richer shades you are looking for and you'll be happier with the results.

My students get tired of hearing me say this (so you won't be alone), but the keys to successful watercolor on Bible paper are *watery washes and drying often*.

Again, practicing with watercolors on Bible paper before you actually take it to your *Legacy Journaling* project will make you more confident. Be sure and check out the *Illuminated Journaling* YouTube channel for lots of inspiration and further instruction on working with watercolors in your Bible.

Colored Pencils and Gamsol/Odorless Mineral Spirits

Colored pencils are another way to quickly and easily add transparent color onto your pages. Since you can read right through them, they give you additional freedom to create illustrations on top of your words, if you like. Almost any set of colored pencils will do; however, I will tell you that this is one place where I have invested a little bit more money. I use Prismacolor Premier™ pencils. Colored pencils are made with the pigment suspended in wax and they blend together when the wax from the two colors becomes softened enough to mix.

With less expensive pencils, you have to do a *lot* of rubbing to get the wax to soften up enough so they can blend because they are made with a very hard wax. The wax in the Prismacolor Premier™ pencils is already softer to begin with, giving you lovely blends much quicker. They become a real time saver if you are going to be working with them a lot. They also enable you to achieve much more subtle shading because you can build up more layers of color with soft wax pencils than you can with hard wax pencils.

I have found a product that can help even inexpensive colored pencils produce similar results to what you can achieve with more expensive brands. You may want to try this out, even if you decide to use the Prismacolor Premier™ pencils, because this technique can give you a really lovely, soft-looking blend that resembles watercolor washes.

To achieve this effect, use Gamsol or Odorless Mineral Spirits and a blending stump to blend your colors together (pictured here). Gamsol is a brand of artist-grade odorless mineral spirits that is more commonly used in the crafting industry—but odorless mineral spirits will also work and are available in the fine art section of your craft store. They may even be available at your local Christian bookstore. This "magical" liquid results in a pretty, almost watercolor-like look since it essentially melts the pencil lines and erases their grainy appearance.

Simply color in your image with colored pencils,and apply Gamsol using blending stumps or Qtips™. I use a circular motion to apply the Gamsol and blend my colored pencils together. The mineral spirits will evaporate and leave no residue on the page. Gamsol will really move the color around on the page, so you may want to go back and color an area again to build up the color. Simply wait until the Gamsol or Odorless Mineral Spirits have evaporated and repeat the color blending process. Note: This technique is made for *regular* colored pencils, *not* watercolor pencils. It is such an easy technique to learn and it really makes a huge impact on your artwork! It is the first technique I teach in my introduction to *Illuminated and Legacy Journaling Live Workshops* because everybody can be successful with these products.

Tracing and Graphite Paper, Metal Ball Stylus

I have added these items to your basic supply list because I have made an assumption that may not be true . . . so please forgive me. I tend to assume that most people have a bit of anxiety about their drawing ability—and these three items help remove that anxiety. So if you are comfortable drawing directly onto your pages, feel free to skip these items.

I love to find images to trace and add onto my pages. My favorite sources of imagery are from Google searches, children's books and the easily accessible coloring books available just about everywhere.

If you find an image on Google that you would like to use, resize it to fit your page and print it out. Then use the tracing paper to create line art from your chosen image. Because tracing paper is translucent, you can see exactly where you want to place the image onto your page. Use a couple of small pieces of washi tape to hold your paper in place. Place the tape on the page so that it forms a hinge for you to lift up during the tracing process, allowing you to check your progress.

Once you have your image on your tracing paper in place, take a piece of graphite paper and place it, shiny side down, in between your image and the Bible page. Graphite paper isn't the same as carbon paper. It is more like the technique you used in elementary school when you scribbled with your pencil on the back of a drawing and then turned it over and transferred the image to another piece of paper. Graphite paper is essentially pencil graphite in paper form. You can erase it, while carbon paper is not *erasable* . . . so be sure to use graphite paper to transfer your images to the pages of your Bible.

After tracing your image onto your Bible page, double check to make sure you have all of the lines you want to use before you remove the tracing paper from the page. You are now ready to begin adding color and detail to your image.

I have also created a couple of products to help you quickly get perfectly proportioned line art onto your Bible pages. *One and Dones* are thematic sets of printed line art that come with graphite paper and a stylus included in the packaging. While there are several sets available, I have created *Stones of Remembrance* themed sets to help you get started as quickly as possible. These are available for purchase at your local Christian bookstore or on my website.

You may also be interested in *Click Prints*, which is a monthly subscription product. Subscribers receive a printable set of line art images delivered each month via email. These *Click Prints* can be printed as many times as you need them and can also be colored, t rimmed out and glued onto your page.

Several videos are available on the *Illuminated Journaling* YouTube Channel to further demonstrate how to use *One and Dones* and *Click Prints* in your *Legacy Journaling* projects.

Let the fun begin!

To Seal Or Not To Seal

That is the question!

Life is filled with mysteries and things that are "unknowable," but this doesn't have to be one of them.

As we discussed, the paper used in Bibles is thin to keep the weight down and is treated with sizing to help it resist dirt and oil from all of the excess handling the pages will endure. This can actually work in your favor, depending on what kind of product you are going to be using on your page.

If you are a *nervous journaler* or if you aren't quite sure what products you may end up using on a page, then you should go ahead and pre-treat your page with clear gesso.

Let me share a little bit about clear gesso. This is one of those products that I really have strong feelings about, so I can only recommend two products that I believe will give you the results that you want. You may have used white gesso in some other craft project. It is typically used as a primer to help paint stick to a surface. White gesso is opaque and chalky. Unless you want to cover something up on your page, you do not want to use white gesso. You want to use clear gesso—and honestly, not just any clear gesso. You want to use a clear gesso that is smooth! Most gesso contains additives that make it gritty. This is called tooth in the art world. It gives whatever you put on top of it something to attach itself to, allowing you to mix and match products on the same canvas. Most product manufacturers have continued to include additives in their clear gesso to also give it tooth. This grittiness becomes a problem when you use it on the pages of your Bible. Because it feels like sandpaper, you can imagine what it does to the nibs of your pens and to your colored pencils—

it destroys them! I have tested most of them and have found only two that I can recommend.

Dina Wakely's Clear Gesso by Ranger
Art Basics Clear Gesso by Prima Marketing

Here are my simple guidelines to prepping pages:

Seal your page with Clear Gesso if:

1. You want to use pens other than Microns on your page.
2. You are a slow writer. The longer your nib is on the paper the more likely your pen is to soak through.
3. You are using wet mediums like dye inks (slow drying inks), gelatos or spray inks.
4. You are going to use watercolor markers.
5. You want to add stamping to your page as most stamp pad inks will bleed through. If you have tested an inkpad and it doesn't bleed, then there is no need to prep your page.
6. You are planning to use texture paste or add additional ink or paint to the page through a stencil.
7. You are a nervous journaler and just want to be sure.

You don't need to seal your page if:

1. You are going to use watercolors.
2. You are only going to be using colored pencils.
3. You are going to use heavy bodied acrylic paint, as it does not bleed through. (Never use bottled craft acrylic paint due to the high water content).

Not so complicated, right? The very best way to be confident that you will get the results you want is to *test, test, test*! I'm beginning to sound like a broken record, right?

Now go forth and seal appropriately.

If you are interested in learning more about these products, we have included additional information, along with tips and tricks for using them and other products, in the companion resource to this book, the **Stones of Remembrance Workbook**.

CHAPTER 4

Selecting The Stones

So I don't mean to stress you out, but you may want to put on a new pot of coffee, or freshen your *Fresca*. While you are getting your beverage of choice, go ahead and pick up a pencil…and more importantly, an eraser!

We're getting to the place where the *rubber meets the road*, as the saying goes. It's time to begin deciding which twelve stones you are going to focus on in your *Legacy Journaling* project. Yes, I know I told you that you could have more than twelve and you certainly can, but you won't know that you need thirteen or fourteen until you do the work of selecting the first twelve. So let's begin with what God thought was important to teach to the children of his chosen people.

> *Hear, O Israel: The Lord our God, the Lord is one. Love the Lord your God with all your heart and with all your soul and with all your strength. These commandments that I give you today are to be on your hearts. Impress them on your children. Talk about them when you sit at home and when you walk along the road, when you lie down and when you get up. Tie them as symbols on your hands and bind them on your*

foreheads. Write them on the doorframes of your houses and on your gates.

Deuteronomy 6:4-9

In Hebrew (שְׁמַע), the word for *listen* or *hear* is **shemá.** This passage in Deuteronomy has become known as the *Shemá*, the fundamental statement of Israel's faith. The teaching of the *Shemá* was to be indelibly imparted to Hebrew children by *constant repetition* so that they would never lose sight of the most important aspects of *who God is* and *how we*

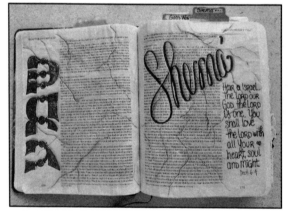

are to relate to Him. I love thinking of Jesus being taught to say the *Shemá* as a young Jewish child. Isn't that a delicious thought? Jesus, who knew his Heavenly Father personally, was taught to say the *shemá* by his earthly father. Once he began his earthly ministry, the Pharisees who were experts in the Jewish law tried to trap him by asking, *"Teacher, which is the most important commandment in the law of Moses?"*[1]

Can't you just see it? The smug look on their faces. They thought they had him backed into a corner. Until Jesus came and paid the price for our sins, the only way to be held righteous was to carefully keep every single law and to offer appropriate sacrifices for failure to keep the law. The Pharisees thought that if Jesus offered one law above another that they could prove that he was a heretic and should not be followed even as a wise rabbi.

Jesus used the words of the *Shemá* that he learned as a child and answered them with, *"you must love the Lord your God with all your heart, all your soul, and all your mind. This is the first and greatest commandment. And second is equally important. 'Love your neighbor as yourself.' The entire law and all the demands of the prophets are based on these two commandments."*

*He just lowered the **boom**!*

He basically said that a simple child is capable of knowing the most important things there are to know about God! I love that and I'm so glad it is true.

Actually, this is what took the stress out of selecting the stones for me. I was getting so tied up in knots trying to make sure I covered all the important things, but then I realized I was stressing out over something that was really much simpler than I was making it out to be. {Unfortunately, over-complication is one of my gifts!]

As you set about deciding what you want to include in your *Legacy Journal*, keep your decision-making filter as un-complicated as possible. God's Word provides everything that we need to know **who God is, what He has done for us** and **how we are to relate to Him**—these journals are meant to be our testimony of God's faithfulness in our lives as we have stood on these truths.

Regardless of where you land on the selection of your stones, I want to encourage you to focus on documenting your experience and testimony in regards to each of the stones. This is something I talk about in my live workshops quite a bit. I do so because as someone who believes that the Bible is God's infallible Word and that it is not in need of any defense by me, I don't want *Legacy Journaling* to become something that is seen as a way of *explaining or defending* it. God's Word does not need my defense . . . *period.*

I am a fan of Charles Spurgeon and am especially fond of

his response to a reporter's question regarding him being a *defender* of God's Word. As only Charles Spurgeon could do, he managed to use a combination of words that were both economical and colorful. He said, *"Defend the Bible? I would rather defend a lion. Unchain it and it will defend itself!"*

Yes and amen.

Brainstorming Your List

My first list was a hot mess—and that is okay. Yours might be too, so just know it in advance and be prepared to go with the flow. We are working on a resource, not a finished product. There is no need for perfection here. Yes, you will probably hear me say that again at least a time or two.

When I began to brainstorm what I would consider using for my *twelve stones of remembrance,* I already had a composition book full of ideas. You know, the one that had paralyzed me? I didn't have enough sense to start with a blank slate, so my book continued to overwhelm me until I put it away. If you have been collecting ideas in a book or in another resource, I suggest not having it out when you sit down to brainstorm your twelve stones. I think you will be more satisfied with your list if you begin with a worksheet that has the following question written at the top, along with nothing but blanks (and lots of them) for you to fill in with your answers:

If I could sit down and tell _____ (name of the person/people the *Legacy Journal* is for) about the most important encounters I (or they) have had with God and His Word, I would talk about _____ :

Let yourself brainstorm. This is personal and there are no wrong answers. And I can't emphasize this enough—*give yourself time to reflect.*

I found that I would think of new things to add to my list while I was doing other things. I let my list stay on my desk for two or three days and would glance over it before I sat down to do my quiet time. I really did want to hear from the Lord and I am my most quiet and listening self after I've studied His Word and have had a few moments of quiet prayer . . . so I refreshed my memory of where I was on making the list right as I began my quiet time.

I added things onto this list like, *my adoption, the moment I realized that loving Jesus wasn't enough and that I needed a Savior, the first time I remember memorizing scripture and having it come to my mind when I needed it, the decision-making process for choosing my career path, getting lost with my cousin trying to walk from one grandparent's house to another, a specific time when finances were so tight and God miraculously provided more than what was needed, mission trips, wanting a child and not having one when all of my friends were becoming mothers, the joy of having a sister, seeing the peace in the eyes of my grandmother when she was* *ready to move on to heaven, having the joy of Weston calling me Mama for the first time...*and the list went on and on.

Even if I had never moved on to creating a *Legacy Journal*, I have to tell you that this was one of the most faith-altering exercises I have ever been involved with—and I recommend it highly for all Christ followers. When you realize exactly how much a legacy of faithfulness has already been in your life up to now, it changes your perspective of where your life is in the present. This is true whether you have only recently dedicated your life to Christ or if you have been walking with him for years. It shattered me . . . in the best way possible.

Brainstorming ideas is a great way to help you discover what is really important, so on your first pass, don't edit yourself. If you think it, write it down. If you have the **Stones of Remembrance Workbook**, use the *Encounters Brainstorming Worksheet* to help you in this process.

Narrowing It Down

You have just created your most valuable resource for this project. If your experience is anything like mine, you haven't finished adding things to it because you will continue to have additional personal encounters come to mind as you work on your project. Just add them to the list—it's never too late.

I still wasn't quite yet ready to pick out my stones, and when I am stumped by a problem, I tend to go into organizational mode. There wouldn't be a clean closet or drawer in my house if I didn't find myself trying to figure out a problem from time to time. There's something about a dilemma that makes me say, "I think that junk drawer needs to be cleaned out!" Are you like that?

Apparently, I am not the only one who has noticed this about me. I had a dear assistant who was leaving to go home on a Friday who said, *"Okay, well I guess I will see you tomorrow!"* I looked up from the papers I was reading and said, *"Don't you mean Monday? It's Friday!"* To which she laughed and said, *"You don't think I'm going to let you rearrange those file drawers all by yourself tomorrow do you? I'd never be able to find anything. Lord knows you are chewing on a problem and if I don't show up here tomorrow, you are going to have torn into those drawers and cleaned them out while you are trying to come up with your solution. I'll see you tomorrow!"*

I guess I am more transparent than I thought!

When I finished my list, rather than clean out a drawer, I decided to organize my answers. You might find this process helpful as well.

I started with three more sheets of paper, each with one of the following as a heading:

Who God Is

What He Has Done For Us

How We Are To Relate To Him

I then took each of the items on my list and added them onto the appropriate page. Some of them went onto more than one page. This isn't an exact science; it really is more about giving yourself some perspective about what you have to work with—and where you may still need to do a bit more thinking. If you are using the **Stones Of Remembrance**

Workbook, you will find these worksheets right after the *En-counters Brainstorming Worksheet.*

As I was transferring my personal encounters over to these new worksheets, I began to realize that I could begin to list *themes* or single word descriptions of the types of things I had added to these new sheets. So I began to write those themes along the bottom of each sheet. I used words like *Salvation, Forgiveness, Dealing With Disappointment, Provision, Holy Spirit, and Obedience etc.*

Then suddenly, I began to feel as if I actually had a start on my twelve *stones of remembrance.*

I started another list on another page . . . you can see why I am a fan of composition books, journals and workbooks. Otherwise, I would have bits and pieces of papers flying everywhere!

This page had twelve blanks on it in the center. I even drew a rough outline of the stacked stones around the blanks. I then rewrote all of my themes around the perimeter of my stacked stones. Like a stonemason trying to fit together the perfect pattern, I began to try out different groupings of themes inside my stack of stones. Here is where your eraser will be your best friend. Create your own set of stacked stones or use the worksheet provided in your workbook.

Again, give yourself some time with this process. I found that with a little contemplation, some of the themes could be combined—like putting *sin and forgiveness* together with *sal-vation.* I found that all of my themes could fit, if I could only be a little creative in my combinations. Remember, we are doing this as an exercise to have a filter to keep the scope of our project doable. No one other than you is going to know if you put a couple of things together that are only loosely con-nected . . . nor will you be bound by these 12 topics alone. I have certainly added things to my project that don't fit neatly into one of these themes, but I needed a place to start. These 12 stones of remembrance helped me do it.

Here is where I landed.

What do you think? Did we end up with similar lists? I bet we're close!

When I sat back and looked at my pile of stones, I felt a sense of great satisfaction. When I reflected back on the purpose of the original pile of stones from the Jordan River, I felt like mine suited its original purpose well. When my children, grandchildren or anyone important to me would ask me what those twelve *stones of remembrance* meant, I could certainly tell them that they were there as a testimony of the faithfulness of God in my life.

For the next twelve mini-chapters, I am going to take each of the stones that I have selected and share a bit about each one. My goal is to give you some context, but also some verses you may choose to use when journaling about your topics. I want to also provide some inspiration in the form of journaling prompts and examples from my own *Legacy Journaling* projects. I hope they become a source of inspiration and spur you on in your own creativity.

Notes

[1] Matthew 22:35-4

Color Photo Gallery

I have chosen to include black and white photos in each of the chapters that contain artwork that I have created for my own Legacy Journaling projects. But I wanted you to be able to see them in greater detail here in the color gallery.

Joshua 4:6-9 pg 9

Baby Bump, Psalm 71:6 pg 23

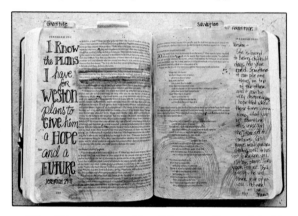

I Know The Plan I Have For Weston, Jeremiah 29:11 pg 24

Shema, Deuteronomy 6:4 pg 62

Charles Spurgeon
pg 64

Where Mercy Meets Grace
2 Corinthians 12:9, pg 84

Hope Poured Out
Philippians 4:6-9, pg 87

What's So Special About Enoch
Genesis 5:21-24 pg 96

Three Months In
Psalm 91, pg 99

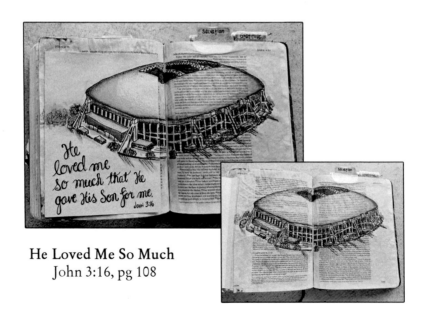

He Loved Me So Much
John 3:16, pg 108

Names of God
Exodus 15:26 pg 120

God Is A Holy Warrior
Psalm 91, pg 122

It Takes Discipline
1 Corinthians 9:27, pg 130

God Is With Her
Psalm 46:5 pg 131

Straighten Your Crown
Matthew 16:19, pg 139

This World Is Not My Home
John 18:36, pg 141

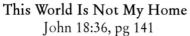

The Holy Spirit
Is My Contractor
1 Corinthians 6:19 pg 149

Plug In
2 Corinthians 13:14, pg 150

May Hope Abound
Romans 5:13, pg 151

Possum Thinking
Psalm 128: 1-2 pg 160

Let's Do Our Homework
James 1:5, pg 162

Whoever Pursues Rightousness
Proverbs 21:21, pg 163

Bag of Chips
Psalm 19:14, pg 172

Heart of Stone/Heart of Flesh
Ezekiel 36:26 pg 173

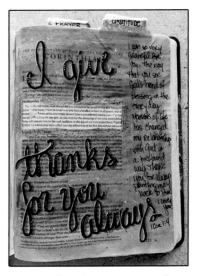

Count Your Blessings
Psalm 118:1, pg 181

I Give Thanks For You Always
1 Corinthians 1:4, pg 183

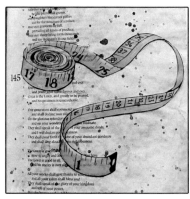

Beyond Measure
Psalm 145:3 pg 190

Ascribe To The Lord
Psalm 96: 8-9, pg 191

Let The Wise Hear
Proverbs 1:5, pg 198

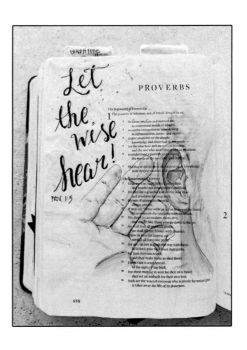

**We Will Pray For
This Child**
James 5:15, pg 200

First Night Jitters
Joshua 4:19-22, pg 209

CHAPTER 5

The Stone of Hope

Let us hold tightly without wavering,
for God can be trusted to keep His promises.
Hebrews 10:23

Don't be afraid, for I am with you.
Don't be discouraged, for I am your God.
I will strengthen you and help you.
I will hold you up with my victorious right hand.
Isaiah 41:10

If we were to return to the bank of the Jordan River and pick out actual stones to go along with our categories, I would be looking for the guy who could pick up the biggest boulder. This category needs a larger than normal stone not because it is more important than all the others, but simply because there are so very many applications for it. In all the Legacy projects I have done, I have dealt with this stone in six different ways—and doubled up with multiple entries in a few as well. Hope encompasses such a broad spectrum of encounters with God, along with the realities that we face when we lose hope and are anxious, discouraged, disappointed or fearful.

Hope /hōp/
> *Noun* 1. A feeling of expectation and desire for a certain thing to happen. 2.a feeling of trust
> *Verb* 1. To want something to happen or be the case

In our family Legacy Bible, I have entries for all the positive aspects of hope and why I know we can trust God to provide us a hope and a future[1]. However, it has also made sense to me to deal with the difficult realities of living here on this earth. We will face disappointments, be discouraged, and in all likelihood, we will know moments of fear or anxiety. I wanted to document how the Lord has met me and members of my family in each of those situations in real and tangible ways. In the future, I believe there will be someone facing disappointment, sadness, fear or anxiety who will draw strength from what they will see in our Bible. I am going to share a couple of them with you. Some that I have included in our Bible are not my stories to tell, so I will keep them private, but I do hope [there's that word] that these examples will help you determine how you want to deal with the *Stone of Hope* in your Legacy Journaling project.

My Journaling

What do you want to be when you grow up?

How many times do we get asked that when we are kids? A ton, right? In all the times that I was asked that question, I always said, "I want to be a Mom." Later, as I contemplated going to college, it finally occurred to me to also think about what career I might want to pursue. Even so, my answer never waivered. I had interchangeable career options ranging from musical therapist to attorney, but I always ended my answer with "and a Mom." I just felt really clear about that one thing. In hindsight, I realize that it was pretty normal for me to just assume I would be a Mom someday, but the fact that I was adopted most likely elevated this desire in my mind. I wanted to be there for a son or a daughter in ways that I didn't experience until I was adopted later as an older child.

I didn't worry about it much. I pursued my career and was neither a musical therapist nor an attorney. I was a missionary and I loved every minute of it, even the hard days. That happens when you know you are right where God intends for you to be. And then one day I looked up and realized that most of my friends were married and instead of going to bridal showers, I was now going to baby showers. And for the first time, I felt a little unsteady about my assumption that I was going to be a Mom. And I didn't like it one bit. So I began a dialogue with God that was not unlike Hannah in 1 Samuel.

I made my request known to God. I prayed, *Lord, I want to be a Mom so badly...please will you grant this request? I know that you answered Hannah and I believe you will answer me. I know that I have been so busy and perhaps haven't been as aware of things that I need to do to be ready to be a good wife and a mother, so just know that I am going to be intentional.*[2]

I turned 30 that year. The young man I had been dating moved away and we grew apart. My heart felt incredibly sad and disappointed. The next spring when Mother's Day came around, I chose not to go to church. Instead, I took my Mom to lunch with my sister and celebrated both of them. I operated under a new premise: if an activity made me feel keenly aware of not being a Mom, I would just avoid it.

I continued to dialogue with God, but with a bit more intensity and a bit less understanding. *Father, I don't understand what you are doing. Why is this one thing I want so seemingly elusive in Your plan for me? Would I be such a terrible Mom that you won't allow me to be responsible for one of your precious ones? I just don't get it.*[3]

That was the year that I began to travel extensively in Russia working in orphanages. And while my heart was still broken and bruised from not having a child of my own, I had the most incredible opportunities to share God's love and goodness with some of the most despairing and hopeless little children in the world. And they loved to hear my story. I would tell them how I had been an orphan too, just like them. I didn't have a father or a mother, but I met my Heavenly Father and became a daughter of the King. If you don't know this, most orphans have stories made up in their minds about being the long lost child of someone famous. I got to sit next to them and introduce them to their Heavenly Father . . . and affirm that they were indeed a Princess or a Prince. I got to look them in the eyes and tell them that they were loved and worthy. I was able to do things for them that a Mom would do and that if they were not adopted in all likelihood, they would never experience on this side of heaven. I brushed and braided their hair. I snuggled them on my lap and made them giggle. And slowly, I felt the absolute sadness of not having a child of my own begin to abate. God's answer to my prayer did not come in the form I had thought it should come, but I could clearly see His hand in this and I began to feel my contentment returning.

I can't say that I stopped wanting to be a mother. I never stopped wanting this, but I began to see how the desire could be fulfilled in non-traditional ways and I wanted to submit myself to God's unique plan for me. He indeed did have a plan for me, plans for good and not for disaster. He gave me hope for my future—and my heart warmed to the anticipation of what He had for me, even if I were to never have a son or a daughter.

Then I met Royce—and later Weston. They both stole my heart. If you've never felt like a part of you was missing, then you may not know exactly what I felt when I was with them. There were just these Royce and Weston-shaped places in my heart and they were the only ones who would fit there. I loved watching Royce be a dad to Weston. And while I always knew that Weston had a mother and I supported and respected her place in his life, he chose to let me have a place there too. And then one Mother's Day—a day that was still very difficult for me—I stopped dreading it. This little boy brought me a card upon which he had marked out the word "Mom" and had written "Mama" instead. His little heart had room for me and he had his own name for me: Mama.

That moment is where mercy met grace . . . and hope flourished.

My Journaling

Kidney failure is scary, but even more so when you don't see it coming. It seemed like Royce was well one day and very sick the next. The first time we went to the hospital, we didn't even know what the problem was . . . he ended up in the ICU. Weston and I were overwhelmed with all the information that was being thrown at us and all the decisions we needed to make on Royce's behalf. Our pastors came in the middle of the night and stood around the bed with us in the ICU as we prayed together. We prayed for God to heal Royce, for wisdom to be applied to this situation and for peace.

The next morning, the nephrologist told us that Royce's kidneys were failing. They said that his toxin levels were so high that, unless something changed, they would have to begin dialysis on him the very next morning. I remember nodding on the outside, but saying "no" on the inside. I didn't know why I had such an aversion to this as the solution at the time, but I did. Weston and I prayed over Royce, asking God to bring his toxin levels down to the point that he didn't need immediate dialysis.

The following morning, the nephrologist came in and said, *Royce's toxin levels have plateaued and we are going to give him a few more hours before we start dialysis, but we still think that tomorrow we will have to start him on dialysis.* I was no longer nodding on the outside, I was convinced that God intended for Royce to leave without having to begin permanent dialysis. We were certainly grateful for the excellent care that he was getting, but we didn't feel peace about the direction. We had prayed for peace and when it was only noticeably absent when the topic of dialysis came up, we began to believe that God had a different plan. So we continued to pray.

The next day brought another visit from the nephrologist. This time she looked puzzled as she looked at his blood work. Her words confirmed that she didn't quite know what to say. *This is very interesting, his toxin levels are decreasing. They still aren't good, but we have no explanation as to why they are going in the right direction because we are not doing anything for him that should be giving us these results. We think we should wait another day to begin dialysis and let us see what his body does.* Now I was back to nodding on the outside. Yes!

This pattern continued for a week. Every day Royce became stronger and we were able to begin telling him what had happened over the past several days. We started guessing how the doctor was going to break the news to us that she wasn't going to have to start dialysis that day, but maybe the next day . . . because that is what she said every single day. She just had no explanation for it, so she continued to expect that the good news wouldn't last. But we knew. We were at peace. And we were far from anxious.

Then the day came when she said she was going to release Royce to go home. Oh happy day!

We knew that we had a long road ahead and we really had no clue what that journey would look like. In the end, God chose to heal Royce by providing him a transplanted kidney—*K. Gray*, as we affectionately call it [short for *Kidney Gray*]. He never had to do hemodialysis. In the end, he was able to do peritoneal dialysis. It is an amazing breakthrough that doesn't have all of the painful side effects of hemodialysis. And it can be done at home. Royce was healthier and stronger because of it, which made him an excellent candidate for a transplant earlier than he would have been had he been a hemodialysis patient.

Looking back, we see that our focus on asking for God to reveal His plan for us by giving us peace (or the lack thereof) was exactly what we needed. We lived and breathed Philippians 4, "Don't worry about anything; instead, pray about everything. Tell God what you need and thank him for all he has done. Then you will experience God's peace, which exceeds anything we can understand. His peace will guard your hearts and minds as you live in Christ Jesus." Yes and amen!

Instead of being overwhelmed with worry and anxiety, we had an abundance of peace that seemed to be poured out on us continuously. Even when those around us would say that the situation was dire, we didn't feel that it was. We knew it was serious. We understood the consequence of kidney failure, but when peace washes over you, there is no fear of what tomorrow may bring.

Creative Walk Through Of My Entries

I love getting to share both of these examples with you because they reflect how the Lord can give us hope in two very different ways.

First of all, I had to walk through many years of learning to trust his heart when I couldn't understand what he was doing. Only through this process could I see the fullness of his plan for me. When it was revealed, it was better than I could have come up with on my own. I wouldn't have missed being Weston's Mama for the world…and I am so glad that God didn't take my demands and say, *Well, I had something better planned for you, but since you can't wait, we'll do it your way!* I rest in that encounter with him on a daily basis. He is trustworthy. He is good. He does have a plan to give me a future and a hope.

The second example demonstrates how we can have hope given to us almost instantaneously and with more abundance than we even knew to ask for.

When Mercy Meets Grace – 2 Corinthians 12:9

A photo that someone shared on Facebook last fall inspired my journal entry for the first encounter. You may have seen it. It is a street sign that indicates the names of the streets are Mercy and Grace. That's a crossroads I'd love to build a house near! I don't know if it is an actual sign or if it was just made up, but it spoke perfectly to the heart of this encounter. So I traced it and created line art for my entry. I think it is such a universal image that I have included it in a couple of sizes in the **Stones of Remembrance One and Dones**. I chose to use watercolors and colored pencils because they are transparent and you can read through them. Also, I really wanted this image to take a prominent space on the page.

Hope Poured Out – Philippians 4

My second entry stumped me for a while. I was research- ing imagery that was focused on the hospital aspect of this story. I even looked at pictures of kidneys . . . so now you know that I have a lot of bad ideas before I find good ones! Then it occurred to me that the most important part of this en- counter was that we felt flooded with peace on a daily basis. If we had a moment where we felt peace was waning, we simply asked—and it was poured over us again in abundance. The only times we didn't feel it were when we were dealing with a solution that was not God's best—and that absence of peace also became our guide. There was so much peace that it stood in stark contrast to those few moments where we didn't feel it. I chose to add an image of water pouring into a pool and still continuing to be poured out. Sometimes it is better to illuminate the feeling with imagery that is more of an analogy than a literal representation.

Inspiration

In each of the following chapters, I will end with some additional inspiration to help you jump-start your own creativity. You will find a list of several verses that I have found useful when journaling about the topic covered in the chapter. It is certainly not a complete concordance, but rather a sampling to get you started. You will also find some topical prompts, or journaling ideas to give you other options for journaling beyond the examples I share from my own projects.

Hope Verses:

Joshua 1:1-9, 2 Chronicles 20:15, Psalm 34:4, Psalm 40:2, Psalm 91:2, Psalm 94:19, Proverbs 31:25, Isaiah 41:10, Isaiah 61:1-4, Jeremiah 29:11, Matthew 6:22, Matthew 6:27, Matthew 11:28-30, Philippians 4:6-7, Hebrews 10:23, 1 Peter 1: 13, 1 Peter 3:15, 1Peter 5:7

Hope Prompts:

1. Journal a long-term encounter you have had with God's Word and the hope that it provided you. I believe that one of the best gifts we can share is an understanding that God is trustworthy, particularly when we are faced with disappointment or discouragement. John 16:33 expresses a difficult truth with a precious promise. *"I have told you all this so*

that you may have peace in me. Here on earth you will have many trials and sorrows. But take heart, because I have **overcome the world***.*" Sometimes the only thing we need to help us hang on and believe is to know that someone else has been there and managed to make it through because God brought them safely to the other side.

2. Take one of the following feelings that seem to come when we don't have hope and address how you have applied the Word of God to help you counteract it: loss of hope, anxiety, discouragement, disappointment or fear.

Notes

[1] Jeremiah 29:11

[2] Personal Journal entry August 1991, Jann Saulsberry

[3] Personal Journal entry May 1993, Jann Saulsberry

has given me permission to take excerpts from her blog and add them to our family *Legacy Bible*. Is it raw and real? Absolutely—and that can give future generations an idea of just how present God will be in the midst of their own moments of deep loss, pain and sadness.

My Journaling

(Excerpted from my sister's blog)

Three months in and our family has begun to encounter real "firsts" without Tod. Tears have flowed collectively and privately, and yet joy and laughter have accompanied those moments as well. I don't understand it other than to know that Jesus is here amongst us and he won't leave . . . and I am grateful.

Blessed be the God and Father of our Lord Jesus Christ, the Father of mercies and God of all comfort; who comforts us in all our affliction so that we maybe able to comfort those who are in any affliction with the comfort with which we ourselves are comforted by God. 2 Corinthians 1:3-5

Since Tod's earthly journey ended and his heavenly one began, God's ability to comfort me while such an ache in my soul exists is nothing short of astounding. My life feels strangely quiet with Tod's absence and memories are visiting more often now. Yet God's Holy Word continues to carry new meaning for me as it reaches into the crevices of my hurting heart with His gentle promises of help and healing, calling me to trust Him even when it doesn't seem real or possible or makes any kind of sense.

God, who revealed himself to me years ago, has relentlessly pursued me during this time of loss and brokenness. His comfort and love has abundantly poured out in ways I could have never imagined, weaving His peace and unearthly joy into this space. That I can feel sorrow and yet melt into a place of peace, or be caught up in a storm of tears and then sense God's grace flooding in, continues to mark this time in my life with the truth that I am being sheltered under God's shadow.

This verse has taken on new meaning for me, *He who dwells in the secret place of the Most High shall abide under the shadow of the Almighty.* (Psalm 91:4) I take heart in this promise of God being purposeful in placing His shadow over me and my children, for a shadow can only be cast when something is standing between you and the burning glare of the sun. God Himself is in that space continually protecting us from the scorching heat of life's offering right now, which could so easily parch our weary souls. But He continues to provide a place of rest and sustenance for us in Him. He truly is our protector and provider, a hiding place that is safe and trustworthy.

As His hope works into my soul, it doesn't remove or lessen the heartache; instead I have found that it couples together with it. Grabbing a hold of each painful moment, mingling it with a quiet, but sure knowing that even in the midst of these circumstances, the promises of God's love and goodness are there ever present and eternal. That stirs a deep sense of gratitude in my heart and each new day that I am given the gift of being with "my people" has become such a precious treasure.[1]

Personal encounters with God have a profound effect on us. This is why I want to encourage you to include personal testimonies in your Legacy Journaling projects when it is appropriate. Certainly, I want to caution you to be considerate, particularly if someone is in the midst of the process. They may not yet be ready to share their very private encounter in a public way. If not, you may want to just add a post-it note to the page where you think the testimony would be appropriate and let it be a reminder to you to add it later when the experience is less raw.

In the final chapter, I will be sharing some additional ideas about how to incorporate life events into your Legacy Journaling Bibles, specifically the ones that don't fall neatly into your framework of stones. But I can suggest that the stone of faithfulness can cover a multitude of events . . . our lives are nothing if they are not a living testimony of the faithfulness of God and our desire to be found faithful.

Creative Walk Through Of My Entries

One of the challenges that I discovered while making the transition from creating personal journaling pages to creating entries that are intended for others to read was that, many times, I needed to include a greater amount of journaling to be sure and communicate the complete context of the entry. In my personal journaling Bibles, I can remind myself of what I learned by simply adding a title or a bit of journaling to the page – but when that doesn't always work well in a legacy project. To give myself more room to work and write, I have chosen to incorporate what I call *tip-ins* (because they *tip into* the page and give you more space to work with). They can be made from anything and then just added to the page with a bit of tape (I prefer washi tape to create a hinge). Most often, I use a piece of cardstock or watercolor paper and add my imagery onto the front of the tip-in and hide my journaling behind it. This chapter's two examples will show you a couple of ways that I have included *tip-ins* and you will find many more examples in the coming chapters. Creating *tip-ins* takes a little planning, but it is worth it. You will find more information on how to create a *tip-in* in the Techniques section of the workbook.

Poof! What's So Special About Enoch?—Genesis 5:24

This *Legacy Journal* project is for a young boy in our family and will be a work in-progress for the next few years. Even when one won't be completed for some time, I love for the recipients to know that I am working on the project for them—and I even like to let them see it, if they are interested in it. In this particular case, when I visit his family, I bring his Bible with me and we look through it together. I love to listen to his thoughts, looking for ways that I can incorporate his observations into this special gift. His mom and dad have been good about sending me notes, letters and prayers that they have written for him, so I am working those onto the pages of his Bible as well.

You can see that I am keeping these early entries in his Bible fun and visually engaging. What little boy doesn't like comic books? The bright yellow, red and purple **poof!** will capture his imagination, and then my simple journaling about what happened to Enoch will hopefully encourage my young friend to be curious about more than the fact that Enoch went **poof!**

I did a Google search for comic book lettering and traced the letters onto a watercolor card *tip-in*. I filled in the letters and background with watercolors, choosing really clear and clean colors that you would find in the pages of a comic book.

Three Months In—Psalm 91:4

When entries are this personal, I try to keep everything as simple as possible. I used a photo of my sister and Tod, printing it out on printable vellum. I created two frames for the photo. The front frame was cut from some shimmery cardstock and the backside was made from white cardstock. I then sandwiched the photo between the two frames with strong double-sided tape. I used a set of stamps and dies[2] to create the flower arrangement for the lower right corner. I then printed out the journaling and attached it to margin of the Bible page. I used a light watercolor wash of a neutral gray to create a simple background and then I attached the *tip-in* and journaling to the page edge with a strip of washi tape.

For more information on using printable transparencies/vellum in your journaling, check out the instructions I provided in the *Creative Walk Through* section of *Chapter 10: The Stone of Our Identity In Christ.*

Faith Verses:

Genesis 5:24, Exodus 34:6, Deuteronomy 7:9, Deuteronomy 11:13, 1 Samuel 12:24, 1 Samuel 26:23, 2 Chronicles 31:12, Nehemiah 9:33, Psalm 25:10, Psalm 26:3, Psalm 31:5, Psalm 32:6, Psalm 36:5, Psalm 40:11, Psalm 52:9, Psalm 85:8,

Psalm 85:11, Psalm 86:11, Psalm 89:37, Psalm 91:4, Psalm
146:6, Proverbs 28:20, Isaiah 11:5, Isaiah 61:8, Lamentations
3:23, Joel 2:23, Zechariah 8:8, Matthew 6:30, Matthew 8:10,
Matthew 9:20, Matthew 9:22, Matthew 14:31, Matthew
15:28, Matthew 17:20, Matthew 25:23, Mark 10:52, Mark
11:22, Luke 8:25, Luke 17:5, Luke 22:32, Acts 11:24, Roman
3:22, Romans 3:28, Romans 5:1, Romans 10:10, Romans
10:17, Romans 12:12, 1 Corinthians 1:9, 1 Corinthians 10:13,
1 Corinthians 15:14, 1 Corinthians 16:13, 2 Corinthians 5:7,
Galatians 2:20, Galatians 3:24, Galatians 3:26, Galatians
5:22, Ephesians 2:8, Ephesians 4:5, 1 Thessalonians 5:24, 2
Thessalonians 3:3, 1 Timothy 4:12, 1 Timothy 6:12, 2 Timothy 2:13, Hebrew 11, Hebrews 11:1, Hebrews 11:6, James
2:17, James 5:15

Faith Prompts:

1. Choose several Bible stories (look at Hebrews 11 for a
   list of stories) and create a Scavenger Hunt of the
   Faithful. Use a similar icon to connect them all together. Always be sure and provide the reference to the
   next story at the bottom of each page.
2. Turn to Hebrews 11 and put a square around the words
   "by faith" every time they appear. Put a watercolor
   wash on the rest of the page (remember you can read
   through transparent watercolor) to highlight just how
   many times "by faith" appears on the page. If your Bible is like mine, it will probably continue on to the second page. Journal your personal thoughts about what
   it means to live "by faith."
3. Hebrews 11 is sometimes known as the *Hall of Fame
   of the Faithful.* Consider creating a family Hall of
   Fame based on people in your family, what you know

about their lives and how they walked out their faith. This is a great way to include ancestors that have already gone home to be with the Lord. If you have pictures of these ancestors, you can print them as I did for my entry on Psalm 91.

Notes

[1] Excerpt from **Between the Plough and the Alter** blog post by
Robyn Bush, http://ploughandaltar.blogspot.com/
[2] *The Sweet Life*, stamps and dies by Papertrey Ink.

CHAPTER 7

The Stone of Salvation

Salvation is found in no one else, for there is no other name
under heaven given to mankind by which we must be saved.
Acts 4:12

I almost always have music playing while I am writing. Just now, I am listening to a song by Tommy Walker called *We Will Remember*[1]. Oh man, it is good! The whole song has become a bit of an anthem for *Legacy Journaling* to me. Here is the part that I can't hear without tears springing to my eyes:

Chorus: *We will remember we will remember*
We will remember the works of Your hands
We will stop and give You praise
For great is Thy faithfulness

Verse 4: *I still remember the day You saved me*
The day I heard You call out my name
You said You loved me and would never leave me
And I've never been the same

Don't you love to remember the day you gave your heart to Jesus like it was yesterday? And don't you echo Tommy's words and say, *"I've never been the same"*? I do—and it is one of my most precious memories from my relationship with Jesus. Even if you don't recall a specific day or time, I'm sure you have special memories of how your life was changed when you asked Jesus to be your Savior.

My Journaling

I was blessed to have been adopted into a family with a long heritage of being Christ followers. Long before I knew that I needed a Savior, I saw the impact that faith had on the lives of my grandparents and parents. It was a natural thing for me to love Jesus, to talk to him daily, to be read Bible stories as part of my book time, to put a quarter and a nickel into the offering plate in "big church" and go to Sunday School and church on Sunday. But the older I got, I began to realize that my parents and grandparents had a different relationship with Jesus than I did. And that didn't set well with me.

I had been an older child when I was adopted and I knew what it was like to *not belong*. I became more and more unsettled in the knowledge that I was once again on the outside. No one said it directly, but I knew by the way they talked about him that they knew something about him that I didn't. I wanted to know what they knew, so I began paying a bit more attention at church and I began to change my prayers to reflect that I wanted to know more about Jesus, as opposed to just listing the things that I needed him to do for me. That is always a good place to start, right?

During the summer I turned nine, my church announced that we were all going to a Billy Graham Crusade. I had no clue what a Crusade was, nor did I know who Billy Graham was, but everyone was so excited that I began to look forward to it unlike anything else. We all met at the church and boarded a bus that drove us to Texas Stadium in Dallas. I'm going to give you a clue to how old I am: Texas Stadium had just been built, but the Cowboys had yet to play a single game there. It was slated to open for the first home game that Fall and they were still completing the final details like the goalposts, which had not yet been installed. I remember noticing the missing goalposts the moment we walked inside and saw the field for the first time.

To a nine-year-old little girl, Texas Stadium was huge! I kept bending over backwards just to be able to see the roof that had a hole in it. My Dad told me ahead of time that the hole in the roof was so that God could watch his favorite team, the Cowboys. Not every word that came out of his mouth was always theologically sound, but that one did seem reasonable to me!

By the time we found our seats, I was convinced that a Crusade was going to be a pretty exciting event. But my interest waned a bit when an old man got up and began to sing a song I had never heard before. That "old man" was George Beverly Shae and he was singing, *How Great Thou Art* . . . only one of the most beloved singers and songs of all times. But I was more fascinated with the rows and rows of people that had filled the stadium. I'm a people-watcher now, and I was a people-watcher back then as well. I passed the time picking out people and making up stories about them in my mind.

I was pretty fidgety. Mom kept telling me to sit still, but I just couldn't. I was just restless. In hindsight, I think my spirit was fighting to retain control of me, but Jesus wasn't going to be denied on that day. Just as Billy Graham got up to speak, I told my Mom that I had to go to the bathroom. My spirit wasn't going down without a fight. Although she was none to happy with me, she took me quickly to the bathroom and we returned to our seats just in time to hear Reverend Graham say, *"Our text for this evening is found in the third chapter of John, verse 16."* As I turned to the book of John, my spirited quieted. I don't remember many of the specifics of what Rev. Graham said during his sermon, but my mind and heart were transfixed. I do recall him saying that we should read John 3:16 like this, *"For God so loved Jann that He sent His only Son, so that if Jann believes in Him she would not perish, but have everlasting life!"*

The light bulb came on and I suddenly understood what I hadn't understood before—*loving Jesus isn't enough*, we have to acknowledge our sin and realize that our sin separates us from God . . . and that we can never do anything to fix our relationship with him on our own. *The only solution is to ask Him to be our Savior.*

At the conclusion of the sermon, Rev Graham invited people who wanted to ask Jesus to come into their hearts to come down to the field and meet with someone who would pray with them. The choir began to sing *Just As I Am*[2]—and as thousands of people began to stream down to the field from all over the stadium, I discovered why we need a song with practically a dozen verses. But my butt was pressed firmly into the stadium seat. I didn't want to tell Mom that I wanted to go down to the field. I kept thinking how unhappy she had been about me needing to go to the bathroom. But Rev. Graham said, *"I see you coming from all over the stadium, but I believe there are still more who don't want to end this night without making things right with their Savior. Don't worry, the busses will wait—slip out of your seat and come on down now!"* I thought he was speaking directly to me! I looked at my Mom and said, *"I have to go down to the field...I'm sorry, but I have to go!"*

Of course, Mom wasn't unhappy with me—her earlier irritation was because she sensed that I had been fighting what the Holy Spirit was doing in my heart, kind of like a child asking for one more glass of water to delay the inevitable moment they must turn the light out and go to bed. She immediately told me to go and that they would be waiting in our seats for me when I came back. I jumped up and ran down those steps to the field. I was going to have the same relationship with Jesus that my family did, and I couldn't wait for it to start!

My heart is so full just remembering how I felt running down those stairs that it is leaking out of my eyes. I hadn't even realized that I had been resisting him, but I certainly understood it in that moment and I wanted to set things right.

A new relationship started with Jesus that night that has been the most significant encounter I have ever had in all my life . . . and I have never been the same.

One of the differences between personal journaling and *Legacy Journaling* is that the story matters. Often in my personal journaling, all I need is the illustration and a few words to capture what is in my heart. When I see the page again, it brings back mind all of the details that were involved in why I chose to create it. Because a *Legacy Journaling Bible* is a record of God's faithfulness in our lives—the details of the story are important. Not all stories are as involved as this personal story of my salvation, and most can be captured in the margins with a few words . . . but don't skimp on the story telling. When I have something that requires more words, I automatically plan to use both margins for the post. I may even create extra space for my journaling by adding some cardstock onto the edge of the opposite page to contain the extended journaling like I did for my entries in the previous chapter. You can see the example of how I used the extra space to record my whole Salvation story near John 3:16 in this photo.

Creative Walk Through Of My Entry

I chose to use an image of **Texas Stadium** because it played such a central role in my Salvation story. I did a Google search on Texas Stadium and found an image that showed the stadium from above. After resizing and printing it out, I traced it (see *Chapter Three* for directions on tracing or the *Basic Techniques* section in your Workbook) and created line art and then transferred it onto my Bible page and onto some watercolor paper to be used as a *tip-in*. I knew I was going to be working with a lot of journaling so I planned on using as big of a *tip-in* as possible and knew that it would cover up part of the artwork on the actual Bible page. The solution was to duplicate part of the illustration onto the card I planned to use to put the journaling behind.

I began by using watercolors to block in the basic colors and then followed up with colored pencil to add shading and detail. I printed out my story and added it behind the card and then used washi tape to create a hinge and added the tip-in to the page making sure that the two illustrations lined up to create one continuous piece of art.

But here are other things that I could have done to tell the same story.

1. Rewritten John 3:16 with my name inserted into it in the margin.
2. Stamped and colored a cross and written my story around the cross.
3. Created an image of steps going down to the field. When I think about that night, my memories are tied to running down those stairs and the relief I felt as I walked back up them to return to my parents (and the busses did wait!)

Inspiration

In addition to Salvation, I have also included the topics of sin, forgiveness, and the Great Commission and sharing our faith in this stone's category. Here are some additional ideas that you may want to consider adding into your *Legacy Journal.*

Salvation

There is an opportunity to use some very powerful imagery regarding our Salvation based on Isaiah 49:16 where God tells us, *"See, I have engraved you on the palms of my hands."* The truth is that Christ's death on the provided the only sacrifice that was sufficient to pay the price for our sins. Not only are our names written in the Lamb's *book of life* [3]when we ask Him to be our Savior, but the nail prints in His hands are there because of my sin. I am inscribed on the palms of His hands—and I am so grateful that I am.

Salvation Verses:

This is certainly not an exhaustive list of verses that pertain to Salvation, but they are a place to start as you consider where you will journal your Salvation stories.

Psalm 27:1, Isaiah 49:16, Ephesians 2:8, Hebrews 2:9, Psalm 80:3, Mark 16:16, John 3:16, John 10:9, Acts 2:21, Acts 4:12, Acts 16:31, Romans 3:25, Romans 5:9-10, Romans 10:9, Romans 10:13, 1 John 5:10-12

Salvation Prompts:

1. Your salvation story
2. The salvation story of your family members.
3. For a child's Bible, have family members write letters in the Bible to the child after the child has made a personal profession of faith.
4. Select one verse about salvation and date stamp it with the day and name of each family member corresponding with their salvation story. This list can grow as the family legacy of faith is walked out in the future.

Sin

Our need for a Savior is the foundation of our faith, and while talking about sin may be difficult, I would certainly encourage you to consider including an entry or two about it in your project. I remember asking Jammy Jane why she loved Jesus so much and her simple answer was one of my first clues that she had something with Jesus I didn't have. She said, *"I love Jesus because He loved me enough to pay for my sins on the cross so that I could be forgiven and spend eternity with Him in heaven."* I couldn't imagine Jammy Jane having committing any sins, but if she had, I was especially grateful that Jesus loved her enough to do that for her. It also raised a question in my own mind: if Jammy Jane needed someone to forgive *her* sins, I was absolutely certain that I did too. Romans 3:23 tells us that *"all have sinned and fall short of the glory of God."* Talking about our need for a Savior in personal terms will have an impact on those who have not yet come to the understanding of their own need.

Sin Verses:

Psalm 51, Isaiah 1:28 Jeremiah 14:7, Acts 2:38, Romans 3:23

Forgiveness

Equally important is our understanding that our sins are forgiven and removed from the eyes of God—covered by the blood of Jesus. I love to use Psalms 103:12 to journal that *"He has removed our sins as far from us as the east is from the west."* A simple compass can provide a visual that gives a connection point to this wonderful truth.

I have found that while most people understand their need for a Savior, the harder part for them to grasp is that forgiveness is available to each of us regardless of what the sin is. Guilt is a powerful emotion and keeps people from living a full and abundant life. I want to communicate my own joy in being forgiven and emphasize that that forgiveness is available to them too. In Psalms 130:4, David reminds us that *with you there is forgiveness, so that we can, with reverence, serve you.*

Forgiveness Verses:

Psalm 103:12, Isaiah 1:18, Isaiah 6:7, Luke 1:77, Acts 10:43, Acts 13:38, Ephesians 1:7, Colossians 1:14, Hebrews 9:22

Sharing Our Faith

I want to encourage my family to be active participants in the Great Commission where Jesus told his disciples, "Therefore, go and make disciples of all the nations, baptizing them in the name of the Father and the Son and the Holy Spirit. Teach these new disciples to obey all the commands I have given you. And be sure of this, I am with you always, even to the end of the age." You may have been involved in outreaches in your community or have traveled on mission trips—these provide excellent ways to share how you have encountered God as you share the good news.

Sharing our Faith Verses:

Isaiah 52:7, Matthew 28:19,-20, Acts 1:7-8

A Special Gift

I am excited to get to share a very special gift with you. As I shared at the beginning of this chapter, I have listened to Tommy Walker's song, *We Will Remember* almost every time that I sat down to work on this book. The lyrics declare that we will remember the things that God has done for us—I believe that is exactly what we are doing when we create *legacy journaling* projects. We asked Tommy if we there were a way for me to share this song with you, and he generously has given us permission to give you a link to a free download of the song! I love his music, and particularly this song, and I think you will too!

If you would like to download *We Will Remember*, use this QR code and your smartphone (you will need a QR Code Reader App) or type in the short URL located under the QR Code to go directly to the page on my website where you can download Tommy's gift to you and to learn more about Tommy's ministry.

This page is not accessible from my website in any other way and since this is a special gift just for you, I would ask that you not share it with others.

I hope you enjoy it!

Download Tommy Walker's
We Will Remember Here

http://q-r.to/baleuV

Notes

[1] *We Will Remember*, Tommy Walker, from **Break Through: Live At Saddleback**

[2] *Just As I Am*, Hymn by Charlotte Elliott

CHAPTER 8

The Stone of God's Character

Be still and know that I am God.
Psalms 46:10

Taste and see that the Lord is great.
Psalm 34:8

This is why you are great, LORD God.
There is no one like you!
2 Samuel 7:22

I love a story that was shared by Max Lucado in his book, ***Experiencing the Heart of Jesus[1].*** He shares that when his younger daughter, Sara, was four years old, she loved to leap from the bed into his arms. She was fearless. She would tell him to move farther back each time and then throw herself with abandon off the bed absolutely confident that he would catch her. When her older sister came in the room, Max suggested that she jump to her sister . . . but Sara would have no part of it. She absolutely refused to jump to her sister. When Max asked her why, Sara told him, *"I only jump into big arms!"*

Isn't that the absolute truth? If we are going to take a leap of faith, we want to know that the arms of God are big enough to catch us! I think that is the essence of why I included the *stone of God's Character* in my stack of memorial stones—I want my family to know that I have jumped into God's big arms so many times and that He has always caught me, keeping me safe. I want them to believe that they can trust Him to catch them as well.

You will find that there are so many ways you can choose to use this particular stone. I have extracted a lot of inspiration for this category from my personal journaling because it gives me an opportunity to share what I have learned about God's character during my personal study times.

One way we can learn about God's character is from the names He gives Himself in the Bible. How do we know that He will provide for us? Because He calls himself Jehovah Jireh [*Our God Is a Gracious Provider,* Genesis 22:13]. How do we know that He can heal us? Because He calls Himself, Jehovah Rapha [*The Lord That Heals You,* Exodus 15:26]. We know that He is our source of peace because He calls Himself Jehovah Shalom [*the Lord is our peace,* Judges 6:24]. If we want to draw attention to His character, a good place to start is with what He says about Himself. I have created a page or two in each of my *Legacy Journaling* Bibles that focus on the Names of God.

Throughout all of my *Legacy Journaling* projects, I strive to share why I am absolutely certain that *God is who He says He is, that He can do what He says He can do, that I am who He says that I am and that I can do what He says I can do.*[2] I was introduced to these four concise statements during a Bible study with Beth Moore called **Believing God** and it changed my interactions with God in a profound way. Now as I study His Word, I try to see how much of it falls into one of those four categories—and I have to say that a vast majority does. Yes, there are *instructions* found in the Ten Commandments and Proverbs, but so many of the *stories* in the Bible inform us about who God is . . . His character.

I have added these four statements almost as a subcategory for this stone because I want to make sure that I am intentional about journaling each of these statements as often as possible. I'll admit that I have a lot of fun working on entries with these focal points. They provide an opportunity for me to do some creative journaling, capturing the imaginations of the little boys (and little girls too, for that matter) in our family. Jesus taught with parables for a reason. We all love a good story from which we can derive meaning. Particularly when I am working on a Legacy Journaling Project for a kiddo, I try to include stories as often as possible. If you can find a way to engage or include them in the story, the impact is even greater.

One of the stories from the Old Testament that I like to use is found in 2 Chronicles 20. It is the story of when the army of the Moabites and Ammonites came against the King Jehoshaphat and the people of Israel—and how God fought the battle for them. By drawing attention to the story, I can draw attention to the characteristics of God that we discover when we study it.

My Journaling

I want to tell you a story . . . a story of what it was like to be the King of Israel and to find out that there were people coming to do battle against you with an army so big that there was no way you could win. The King's name was Jehoshaphat. You know how Uncle Oscar always says, "jumpin' Jehoshaphat?" Well, that's where he got that name! Now King Jehoshaphat knew just what to do—he went to the Temple and had a very serious conversation with God. He said, "God, I know that You didn't let us beat these people and throw them out of this land only to let us lose to them this time. You have told us that whenever we are in trouble, we can come to you. Well, we're in big trouble! We are power-less before these armies. We don't know what to do, but we are looking to you for help." And then he listened.

When God spoke, this is what He said: "Do not be afraid. Do not be discouraged by this mighty army because this is not your fight. **This is my fight***! Tomorrow, you will see them coming up through the valley, but you are not to do anything.* **Just take your positions and stand still . . . and wait to see what I will do.**

As the people went out to meet the army, King Jehoshaphat reminded them "Believe in the Lord your God and you will be able to stand firm." The people trusted God and they even started singing. Can you imagine what the other army thought when they heard the soldiers and the people of Israel singing? They sang, "Give thanks to the Lord, his faithful love endures forever!" And as they sang, they stood still. I bet

that freaked the other army out even more! It must have be-
cause the Bible says that while the people were singing, the
invading armies began to fight each other! Can you believe
that?

When all the dust cleared, there wasn't even one soldier
left alive from the army that had come to do battle with King
Jehoshaphat and the people of Israel! And not only that, but
apparently the soldiers that died that day were really rich be-
cause when the King and his men went to pick up the plunder,
there was too much for them to carry. It took them three days
to collect it all!

God can fight battles that we can't ever imagine winning.
Know that He is always on your side and don't ever be afraid.
He will take care of you!

Creative Walk Through Of My Entries

Names of God

As I mentioned before, I usually create several pages like
this in each of my Legacy Journaling projects. There are so
many times that God introduces Himself to us by a name that
emphasizes a trait of His character. I don't know Hebrew, nor
is it likely that anyone other than my nephew, Tyler, would
actually be able to read the Hebrew name—but I still wanted
to give the names the *look* of Hebrew. When I created this
page for the first time in one of my personal Bibles, I took the
time to create a font that turned our regular alphabet into letters that have similar components to what you see in the Hebrew alphabet. I had so many people ask to use it that I ended

up including it in our first set of **One and Dones**, called *Icons of the Faith*. I have also included a version of this alphabet in your workbook in slightly different sizes to give you more options for using it.

I traced the larger title, *Names of God*, over the body of the text and then used colored pencils and Gamsol (sometimes called Odorless Mineral Spirits) to blend the reds, yellow and oranges together to create an ombre effect. I did not use watercolor except to just do a light wash over the background.

For the individual names, I traced the names in the smaller font and then used a thicker (08 or 1) Micron pen to fill them in. When filling these words in, it is particularly important to use a pen that really resists bleeding as you will be going slower than you would if you were just using your normal handwriting. I then wrote the reference verse for those names below it with a fine point (005) Micron pen. I have provided you several names of God in the Inspiration section—it will not be exhaustive, but it will give you a place to start.

Other things that you could do with the Names of God include:

1. Create a scavenger hunt by starting a page with one name with which God introduces Himself and then let that lead you to another name, which will lead to the next name. This would allow you to keep adding names without feeling that you have to get them all done on one page.
2. You may just want to deal with one name on the page where God first uses it to identify Himself. This is similar to the scavenger hunt, but it doesn't lead to another page—it just stands alone.

God As A Holy Warrior

I thought that there were several really important points to be made with this story. First, King Jehoshaphat knew that the only way they were going to win was if God helped them. Secondly, God's instructed them to not be afraid and let Him do the fighting, specifically telling them to just stand still. Next, the people did what God told them to do—*and* they sang praises to God as the enemy marched towards them with intentions to kill them. Then God caused the soldiers from the enemy army to become confused and begin fighting each other until they all died. And finally, there was a lot of *plunder!*

All of this is going to engage the imagination of a child, so I created a little pocket on the page and slipped a storybook that tells about King Jehoshaphat. I used some texture paste and a stencil to make the front of the storybook resemble an ancient wall and handwrote the journaling and stamped small illustrations on each page. I also stamped a stonewall background stamp in the margins of both sides of the pages (remember to use clear gesso before stamping to avoid the stamped image bleeding through to the other side). The focus of this page is the storybook, so I kept everything else very simple.

Inspiration

I realize there are so many types of entries that you may be inspired to create focusing around God's Names or His Character. I am going to give you a list of a few of the ones that I have used in various projects. These lists are certainly not all inclusive but I hope they will give you a place to start.

Names of God Verses:

Jehovah Jireh: The Lord will provide, Genesis 22:13
Jehovah Rapha: The Lord that heals you, Exodus 15:26
Jehovah Shammah: The Lord is present, Ezekiel 48:35
Jehovah Shalom: The Lord is our peace, Judges 6:24
Jehovah Nissi: The Lord is our banner, Exodus 17:8,15
Jehovah Raah: The Lord is my shepherd, Psalm 23
Jehovah Tsidkeu: The Lord is our righteousness,
                    Jeremiah 23:6
Adonai: God Almighty, Exodus 6:3
Ehyeh asher Ehyeh: I Am that I am, Exodus 3:14
Elohim: Strong One, Genesis 1:1
El Elyon: God Most High, Genesis 14:19
El Shaddai: Lord God Almighty, Genesis 17:1
Yahweh: LORD, Exodus 3:15

God's Character Verses:

Abounding In Love: Joel 2:13, 1 John 4:8
Compassionate: Joel 2:13, Psalms 86:15
Deliverer: Exodus 2:23-25, Psalm 40:17, Psalm 140:7
Faithful and True: Revelations 19:11, Exodus 34:6,
                    Deuteronomy 7:9
Fierce: Deuteronomy 13:17
Fighter: Joshua 23:10
Gracious: Exodus 34:6, 2 Chronicles 30:9
Holy: 1 Peter 1:16, Leviticus 19:2
Jealous: Exodus 20:5, Exodus 34:14, Joshua 24:19
Just: Job 9:19
Kind: Titus 3:4, Romans 2:4

Majestic: Exodus 15:11, 2 Peter 1:17

Merciful: Luke 6:36, Daniel 9:9

Perfect: 2 Samuel 22:31, Deuteronomy 32:4,
        Job 36:4, Matthew 5:48

Powerful: Joshua 4:24, Exodus 4-14, Psalm 29:4,
        Psalm 18:30

Promise Keeper: Genesis 21:1, Numbers 23:19

Refuge: Psalm 91:2, Psalm 62:8

Rock: Deuteronomy 32:4

Slow To Anger: Nahum 1:3, Jonah 4:2, Joel 2:13

Steadfast: Lamentations 3:22-23

Tender: Luke 1:78, Isaiah 63:15

Wise: Romans 16:27, James 1:5

God's Character Prompts:

1. Take a characteristic of God and journal about the ways you have encountered it in your life.
2. On the pages that are meant to engage a younger child, insert a blank piece of paper for them to draw their own response to the story.
3. Write a note next to a verse that has a characteristic of God, but also describes a family member who exhibits this particular characteristic in their own life. Let that become part of the legacy of faithfulness that is passed down from one generation to the next. You might add a picture of the person as a *tip in* or print it out on a clear label and add it into the margin.
4. Create stories that insert the child into the middle of the story or provide questions they can answer after reading the story. I use this as an opportunity to help

them begin journaling for themselves. Even if you are working on a Bible that will not be given to them until later, you can build anticipation for it by letting them participate in it as you make it.

5. Have family members write a paragraph or two about one of the Names of God that they love—and then create a *tip in* with their picture on one side and their note on the backside. Attach the *tip in* near a verse that declares that particular trait of God's Character.

Notes

[1] *Experiencing the Heart of Jesus*, by Max Lucado, Thomas Nelson Publishers

[2] *Believing God*, by Beth Moore, Lifeway Publications

CHAPTER 9

The Stone of God's Word

*Study this **Book of Instruction** continually. Meditate on it day and night so you will be sure to obey everything written in it. Only then will you prosper and succeed in all you do.*
Joshua 1:8

*For the **word of God** is alive and powerful. It is sharper than the sharpest two-edged sword, cutting between soul and spirit, between joint and marrow. It exposes our innermost thoughts and desires.*
Hebrews 4:12

Professional ballerinas at the height of their physical abilities start every day the same way: in class. In fact, they begin every day the same way they did when they were beginners: at the barre.

They begin with small pliés in first position and then progress on to all the remaining positions, always checking to see how their exercises look in the mirror. It is a chance for the foundational movements and shapes of ballet to be observed in isolation. If a ballerina checks them every day, they can't go too far off the rails. Small corrections are easier to make than large ones, so attention to detail in class serves to help the ballerina give her best performance on stage.

They warm up and stretch. They also practice the skill of learning new things. Guest teachers call out different combinations and the ballerina must remember the instructions and recreate the teacher's words with her body. The steps become more difficult as each class progresses.

When her body is warmed up, the class moves to the center of the room...away from the safety of the barre. Now the ballerina must balance on her own. In the center of the room, the steps become more like they will be when she takes the stage. She moves through a series of turns, jumps and combinations of steps designed to move her across the floor, but even now, her attention is focused on her reflection in the mirror as she examines each movement with a critical eye. Are her feet

turned out enough? Are her arms in the correct position and do they form beautiful lines? Only after the rigors of class is she ready to go on to her daily schedule of rehearsals and perhaps even a performance.

Our daily quiet time requires this same sort of discipline and attention in order to prepare us for what our day holds. Whether we are headed into a routine day or one that will require us to be on the stage for the entire world to see, time in God's Word prepares us for whatever the day holds. It allows us to receive small corrections so that we can perfect how to walk out our faith. God's Word provides our instruction, but it is our daily discipline of spending time in it that creates an environment of moving the truth it contains from our head to our hearts.

Create Entries That Apply God's Word

I have mentioned that I use the *twelve stones of remembrance* as a loose framework to guide my journaling decisions. Allow me to share an application of this concept. One of my *Legacy Journaling* projects is for a young family member. I haven't given it to her yet as I will continue working on it as she grows up. I am creating entries that I hope will encourage her walk with the Lord when she is out on her own and will no doubt run into a rough patch. One of the things that most young women deal with at some point in their lives is an issue with self-confidence. I have actually entered several entries into this project to address how encountering God's Word in these situations can change our perspective and give us confidence. I share another similar entry in the *Stone of Who We Are In Christ* chapter. These kinds of entries are testimonials, specifically sharing personal experiences where God's Word has encouraged me— and how I hope that it will encourage her too!

My Journaling

Sometimes trying new things is scary. Honestly, I hate learning new things in front of other people. I would much rather go practice it in private and then reveal my new skill after I have passed the awkward stage. At the heart of this preference is my desire to not look foolish in public. Have you ever felt this way? I bet you have—it is a pretty natural feeling. But here is a verse that has helped to change my perspective. God wants us to have confidence. His definition of failure and foolishness is much different than ours. When He has asked us to learn something new, He says that He will be with us. I love Psalms 46:5 in the English Standard Version of the Bible, **"God is in her, she cannot fail."** Wow! Does that mean that I will nail it the first time? Probably not…but God would only think I had failed if I hadn't tried. I need to remember that He is with me—and that the only opinion I should care about is **HIS**!

Creative Walk Through Of My Entries

The two entries that I have chosen to share with you are great examples of how you can choose to put a lot of effort into a page or you can do something that is simpler—but still packs a lot of punch. I actually love doing both and hope these entries will help you feel the freedom to do whatever works best for you. Be sure and give yourself permission to try new things, but never stress yourself out thinking that the only good entry is a page that takes you several hours to complete!

It Takes Discipline 1 Corinthians 9:27

One of the fun things about creating a *Legacy Bible* for a particular person is that you can incorporate entries that are focused on things specifically important to them. Our goal is the effective communication of how our relationship with God has had an impact on the course of our lives. There is no better way to do that than to use illustrations and examples that will engage their heart and mind. That is why I chose to use the analogy between the daily discipline of ballet class and our daily quiet time. Because the recipient of this Bible was already very familiar with the discipline of ballet class, I didn't need to belabor the analogy . . . a simple title reflecting the comparison was enough.

The verse I used really reflects the way an athlete is determined to discipline their body on a daily basis. It would work for so many other people as well whose interests include sports of all types. I have used this verse for other *Legacy* projects where I was working on a Bible for my son who loves football, and for my niece who played competitive volleyball in high school.

To create the image for this entry, I searched on both Google and Pinterest for the term *old ballet shoes.* I really wanted some beat up shoes that had clearly been well used—and then I had the idea of resting them on the Bible to tie the two together. Even though I did a pretty extensive search, I couldn't find exactly what I was looking for, so I needed to get a little creative. I chose a photo as my reference that showed the shoes from an angle, and I also grabbed a picture of a book that looked like it had been taken from the same angle as the shoes. I resized them to be in right proportion with each other and printed them out (you can resize photos in Word, so you don't necessarily have to have photo-editing software).

HOW TO COMBINE TWO IMAGES:

I started with the ballet shoes because they were in front and traced them onto my tracing paper. Then, I aligned the traced shoes over the image of the book and only traced the parts that were not covered by the ballet shoes. My finished image made it look like the ballet shoes were resting on the Bible. This is one of my favorite reasons to love the tracing technique—*you really can have custom designed images and you still don't have to be able to draw!* For more information on how to create customizable images, refer to the *Techniques Section* of your **Stones of Remembrance Workbook**.

God Is With Her Psalm 46:5

I used a watercolor card to insert this entry. This was a quick and easy entry where I stamped the image onto the card and did some very loose watercolor. I added my journaling to the back of the card. I especially like using this method on entries in those Legacy Journaling Bibles in which I think the recipient will enjoy continuing to journal on their own. That way, my journaling stays self-contained and they still have room to add their own thoughts onto the same page.

Journaling Tip: When the focus is on the *tip in* element, create a simple background in a contrasting color to the card. Contrasting colors will make the *tip in* pop off the page.

Inspiration

There are so many aspects of God's Word that you may want to illuminate in your *Legacy Project*. My entry focused on the *discipline* of spending time in God's Word on a daily basis, but you may want to focus on the *reliability of scrip-*

ture (Isaiah 40:8 or Luke 1:37), *instructional value* (Hebrews 4:12, Proverbs 1:3 or Ezra 7:10), or even how knowing that God's Word gives us authority to live out our daily lives (Hosea 6:3 or Joshua 1:8).

God's Word Verses:

Exodus 18:20, Exodus 32:16, Exodus 34:27, Deuteronomy 4:40, Deuteronomy 29:29, Deuteronomy 30:10, Joshua 1:8, Ezra 7:10, Nehemiah 8:12, Proverbs 1:3, Isaiah 8:20, Isaiah 40:8, Jeremiah 15:16, Hosea 6:3, Matthew 4:4, Matthew 13:23, Luke 1:37, Luke 8:11, 1 Corinthians 9:27, Ephesians 5:26, Ephesians 6:17, Hebrews 4:12, Hebrews 8:10

God's Word Prompts:

1. Isaiah 40:8 is a lovely verse to use with floral imagery. The focus of the verse is that the beauty we see in nature (grass and flowers) is destined to fade, but the Word of the Lord endures forever. Consider simply rewriting this verse framed in flowers and share what draws you to the Word.
2. Create a scavenger hunt with your favorite stories in the Bible. Start on a verse that speaks to the wisdom of knowing what is contained in the Bible and then give the first reference for a favorite story. When they turn to that reference, you can have an illustration or a note that explains why you like it or what you learned from it—along with the next reference for the next verse. This is a great way to be able to keep adding to a Leg-

acy Project over time. If you are doing it for a child, you might make this a scavenger hunt of their favorite Bible stories and share why they seemed to like it when they were young. When they are older, it will provide them a glimpse into their early interactions with God and His Word.

3. Consider taking a book of the Bible that has had a significant influence on the way you interact with God and journal your way through it. For instance, take Proverbs and select at least one verse from every chapter and highlight the power of applying the wisdom found there into your life. Proverbs has 31 chapters, so you might suggest to the recipient that they read a chapter a day—with you providing a note of commentary from your own study of the book.

4. Ephesians 6:13-17 encourages us to put on the full armor of God. Create an illustration of each of the elements of the armor—the belt of truth, the body armor of righteousness, the shoes of peace, the shield of faith, the helmet of salvation and the sword of the spirit, which is the *Word of God.*

CHAPTER 10

The Stone of Our Identity In Christ

For we are all children of God by Faith in Jesus Christ!
Galatians 3:26

*For we are His workmanship, created in
Christ Jesus for good works.*
Ephesians 2:10

*Once you had no identity as a people;
now you are God's people.*
1 Peter 2:10

When we step into our new life in Christ, we are blessed beyond measure . . . *but we are a still a mess.* We're a mess because we are broken, imperfect people who are sinners. But the good news is that we are broken and imperfect people covered by the blood of Christ and therefore covered by His grace and mercy.

Can we just stop and say a big *thank you* [or *hallelujah!* if you are so inclined] for that amazing fact!

Does that mean we stop sinning? No. Do bad things stop happening to us? Absolutely not! Have we entered into the most life-changing relationship we will have in life! Without a doubt! But it takes work—what theologians call the sanctification process. And we would be entering that process with one hand tied behind our backs if we don't understand what God's Word says is now true about us.

When we become followers of Christ, God doesn't take away our propensity to sin—He takes away the eternal consequence from it, calling us into a deeply personal relationship that challenges us to become like Him. *He calls us to be Holy, because He is Holy.[1]* That is pretty serious!

But if we truly understand who we are in Christ, we have access to everything we need not only to survive, but also to thrive.

Can you tell that I am passionate about this particular stone? I am. I know from personal experience what it means to not have completely grasped the significance of my identity in Christ, as well as how dramatically my relationship with Him changed when I did. It is the thing that brought me to the point where I wanted to give God access to all of my brokenness so that He could bring about a redemptive work in my life. Oh don't get me wrong—I'm still a mess. But I'm a mess who knows that I am a daughter of the King . . . and do you know what that makes me? A Princess!

When I am working on a *Legacy Project* for a child, this is how I like to introduce what it means to be a child of the one True King. It is an analogy they will grasp. It will even help launch them into an early understanding of what being a Christ follower means in terms of day-to-day living.

Obviously, if you are working on a project for a young man you can adapt your entry accordingly.

My Journaling

Being a princess is hard work. You need to learn to walk so you can keep your crown straight. You have to be compassionate towards those who have not yet been adopted into the Kingdom family. You need to learn to act with grace and mercy. There is a lot to learn—and God's Word is my *How To Be A Princess Handbook.*

Wherever a princess goes, she represents her Father. She needs to act like He would act. If she sees a problem that needs to be fixed, she needs to fix it as her Father would. As a princess, she has the authority to act on behalf of the King. Do you know what that means? It means because she is His daughter, He has given her the right to speak into certain situations . . . and what she says is just as if the King has said it Himself. That is a lot of power!

We have that same power given to us by our Heavenly Father when we are adopted into His eternal family. Jesus told His disciples that *I will give you the keys of the Kingdom of Heaven. Whatever you forbid on earth will be forbidden in heaven, and whatever you permit on earth will be permitted in heaven.*² No doubt Satan will come and cause problems, but because you are a daughter of the King, you have the authority to forbid him to mess with you. When you tell him that he must leave you alone, he has to obey because as much as he hates it, he is subject to the authority of the King—and you speak with His authority.

So straighten your crown and tell him to get lost!

Before I move on, I do want to acknowledge the one thing that you may have found missing from my *Straighten Your Crown* journaling. Yes, we do have authority to speak on behalf of our Father in heaven, but it should always be tempered by the fact that we can only speak what we have learned from the Father through His Word. Additionally, we also need to not just assume that what we say—even if it is in alignment with God's Word—is necessarily the ultimate plan God has for any given situation. We speak and ask the Holy Spirit to show us how to continue speaking. I don't include this in the Crown journaling because, while it is absolutely imperative that we act under the power of the Holy Spirit, I have found that I can deal with it more directly in other journaling that I do for the *Stone of the Holy Spirit*. Be sure and check out that chapter for a clearer description of how I choose to share the role of the Holy Spirit in our authority as children of the King.

One other thing I have chosen to communicate about our identity in Christ is that we are Kingdom citizens living in a foreign land. This world is not our eternal home and there is a lot about it that just doesn't make sense. Jesus told His followers that, "My Kingdom is not of this world." [3] And Peter reinforced this truth when he cautioned the church to live in "reverent fear of him [your Heavenly Father] during your time here as ." [4]

I want to stay away from current politics, but there are no other words to use to describe us other than aliens or foreigners. This is not a bad thing; it is something we have to understand in order to live the life God intends for us to live. Take, for instance, the fact that our language is different. We may use words that are spelled the same and sound the same as those around us, but they can have vastly different meanings for a world citizen than for a Kingdom citizen. We can get into trouble if we don't remember that!

My Journaling

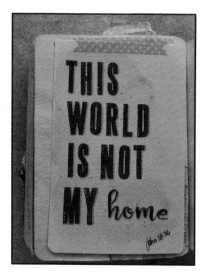

After graduate school, I had a wonderful roommate named Isobel. She was from Scotland and was just an absolutely delightful friend and roomie. She was from the Isle of Lewis, so her brogue was just that much stronger. I loved her accent! I always tried to find excuses to have her pray before our meals just so I could listen to how she addressed her Heavenly Father. I think He probably liked hearing the way she pronounced His name too. And even though we both spoke English, I must say that we had some major miscommunications on several occasions because while our words sounded the same, they certainly didn't mean the same things!

One night, we were going out to dinner with a group of singles from another church. Isobel called to ask me what I thought she should wear. I had just gotten off the phone after asking our friend—who was a member of the group and the one who had invited us—that very question. So I just shared what I had been told, *"Tasha said we should definitely wear pants. They are thinking we might go ice skating afterwards and we don't want to be freezing if we do."* There was a long pause on the other end of the phone and then in a very un-Isobel like voice, she replied, *"Of course I'm going to wear pants! What kind of singles group is it if they only wear pants if they are going ice skating!"* I honestly had no idea why she was suddenly so negative about this group to which we had never been. Only later did we figure it out. In Scotland, the only time they use the word *pants* is when they are talking about underwear . . . otherwise they say *slacks* or *trousers.* If this was a singles group who needed reminding to put their undies on, she was rightly concerned! I still laugh about that misunderstanding.

As followers of Christ, we can get ourselves into the same pickle if we don't remember that our definition for words may be different than the rest of the world in which we live. Some words that sound the same, but have different meanings are: beauty, success, happiness, joy, contentment, wealth, peace, hope, power and authority. Look to the way God's Word— not the world—defines these words and you will never be confused.

Creative Walk Through Of My Entries

Both of these entries use *tip-ins,* a strategy that I love to use when I have significant journaling to include. The one aspect of using tip-ins that I haven't addressed so far is what to do with the background page when the majority of the illustration will be handled on the *tip-in* itself. I typically will use a watercolor wash that is a bit of a contrast to the artwork on the *tip-in* to help the *tip-in* be more eye-catching. When I am creating a simple background like this, I usually will paint the whole page but leave the actual verses I am focusing on blank. To draw a bit more attention to the verses, I will sometimes darken the area around them with colored pencil (it is still transparent) and add a bit of doodling with a white gel pen or a bit of metallic paint to form a bit of a frame. A finishing touch would be a few splatters of watercolor.

Straighten Your Crown—Matthew 16:19

You are probably familiar with the image I used of the little girl and her crown because it has been passed around on *Facebook, Instagram* and *Twitter* for the past couple of years. I loved it from the first time I saw it, so much so that I put a copy of it in my inspiration folder on my computer. I have done a very extensive search to find the originator of this particular photograph, but like most memes, the creator has been lost in all of the reposting.

I printed the image out onto a printable transparency—you may have to search for them online. On occasion, I have found them at local office supply stores, but since nobody uses overhead projectors anymore, they are a little harder to find. Let the print dry thoroughly, especially if you print from an ink-jet printer. Once it is dry, turn it upside down so that you are working on the *backside* of the transparency. (You can tell which is which by looking at the words. When you have the backside facing up, your words will be backwards.). Take a sheet of double-sided adhesive and roll it carefully onto the back of the transparency. (You can also paint gilding glue all over the surface of the backside—just be certain to keep it even and not to miss any spots). Remove the protective sheet from the other side of the adhesive and add gilding flakes all over the backside. When you have it completely covered, use a stiff brush to brush away all the flakes that do not stick to the adhesive. Turn your transparency over. You should have added a bit of metallic shimmer behind your print that enhances the regal look of this little girl. *Note*: You must use *gilding flakes* for this technique. You cannot use heat transfer foil. The metallic finish will be on the wrong side and will not give you the effect you are looking for.

Once I had finished gilding the image, I added a piece of cardstock behind it to make the *tip-in*. My journaling is attached to the back of that card. I simply did a light watercolor wash to the Bible page after outlining the passage of scripture. My finishing touch was to flick a few specks of metallic watercolor onto the background to tie in with the gilding flakes used on the meme card.

This World Is Not My Home—John 18:36

I traced an image of the globe onto the page and added watercolor washes to it and the background. You will find the globe image in your workbook along with a similar text treatment of the words found on the *tip-in*. I did not add any detail with colored pencils to the globe because I liked the loose look of the watercolor. I did finish it by outlining it with a Micron pen (08 nib).

I took a watercolor *tip-in* card and stamped the words, THIS IS NOT MY HOME, with a stamp set that just has the outlines. I then painted in the words with bright colors to contrast with the blues and greens from the globe. The stamps I used are no longer available, so I have recreated something similar for you in your workbook if you want to create a similar look to this project entry. I then printed my journaling from the computer (resizing to fit behind the card) and attached them both to the edge of the page.

Inspiration

Identity in Christ Verses:

Matthew 16:19, Matthew 21:21, John 15:15, John 18:36, Romans 8, 2 Corinthians 5:1-8, 2 Corinthians 5:17, Galatians 3:26, Ephesians 1, Ephesians 2:8, Ephesians 2:19, Titus 3:4-7, Hebrews 11:13, 1 Peter 1:17, 1 Peter 1:18, 1 Peter 2:11

Identity in Christ Prompts:

1. Create an entry where you compare and contrast the language of heaven versus the language of this world. Maybe create a "dictionary" that holds these various words in the margin in such a way that you can add to it over the course of time.
2. Share a story about what it means to be part of your family. Then draw the comparison to what it means to be part of God's family. It is always helpful to start with a familiar concept and then transfer what we know about it to the new idea or concept.
3. Create a page that has a beautiful butterfly on it and journal about the fact that we are made into new creatures when we become Christ followers. Based on 2 Corinthians 5:17.
4. If you are creating this for a child as they are growing up, document specific times when they began to act and sound more like citizens of heaven than citizens of this earth. For instance, perhaps they stood up to a bully on behalf of a friend, or they chose to do the right thing even when no one was looking. These entries will reinforce how we change as a result of having Christ as the center of our lives.

Notes

[1] 1 Peter 1:16, New Living Translation, Tyndale House Publisher
[2] Matthew 16:19, New Living Translation, Tyndale House Publisher
[3] John 18:36, New Living Translation, Tyndale House Publishers
[4] 1 Peter 1:17, New Living Translation, Tyndale House Publishers

CHAPTER 11

The Stone of The Holy Spirit

But the Advocate, the Holy Spirit, whom the Father will send in my name, will teach you all things and will remind you of everything I have said to you.
John 14:26

But you will receive power when the Holy Spirit comes on you; and you will be my witnesses in Jerusalem, and in all Judea and Samaria, and to the ends of the earth."
Acts 1:8

He saved us, not because of righteous things we had done, but because of his mercy. He saved us through the washing of rebirth and renewal by the Holy Spirit,
Titus 3:5

But the fruit of the Spirit is love, joy, peace, forbearance, kindness, goodness, faithfulness, gentleness and self-control. Against such things there is no law.
Galatians 5:22-23

I realize that I have given you an abundance of verses to ponder before we even begin, but I just couldn't leave any of them out! The stone of the Holy Spirit is rather complex, and yet it so very pivotal to our understanding of how we can become the people God intends us to be. It is also vitally important to our *Legacy Journaling* projects.

The Holy Spirit plays many roles in our lives. Before we begin our relationship with Jesus, it is the Holy Spirit who causes us to realize we need a Savior. Afterwards, the Holy Spirit takes up residence in our hearts and begins the process of sanctification, which just means that He works within us to make us more Holy. But that is only the beginning of what the Spirit does for us. He is our *Comforter*, *Guide*, the *Revealer of Truth*, the *One Who Empowers Us*, and the *Giver of Gifts*.

I talk about the Holy Spirit quite a bit in my journaling because I have come to have such an intimate relationship with Him that I want my family to know Him just as intimately. Don't get me wrong; I didn't say that we have an easy relationship . . . that just wouldn't be true. The difficulty lies with me, not Him. I'm the stubborn one—the one who for many years had a tendency to say, *"Thanks for your help, but I've got this!"* only to have to swallow my pride and ask for His help to get me out of the mess that my *"I've got this!"* got me into. Can you relate?

I like to use 1 Corinthians 6:19 to share two very important aspects of the Holy Spirit. The first is what it has meant in my life to have the Holy Spirit come and reside in my heart—to make my heart His home. And secondly, it allows me to talk about the work that He does to make me more holy. "Do you not know that your bodies are temples of the Holy Spirit, who is in you, whom you have received from God? You are not your own."

 In some ways, the Holy Spirit is the General Contractor who comes and

lives in your house while He supervises the renovation process. Have you ever had a reno job done? If not, let me summarize. It is always messier than you ever thought it would be, and it will cost you twice as much as you planned. But when it is done, you are so glad you had the work done!

Likewise, as the homeowner of my body, it never fails that when I think we are going to be working on one room, instead the Holy Spirit starts knocking down walls and changing the whole floor plan! The truth is that my opinion is never as informed as His. He knows where the problem areas are and instead of just covering them up with some wallpaper and a coat of paint, He repairs the structural problems. I may 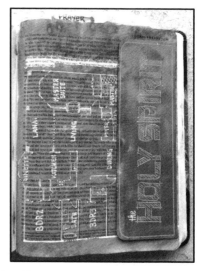 not have even known just how badly the work needed to be done until I see what was behind the walls and under the floorboards.

My best advice? Let Him have His way. Yes, it is hard work, but it has always been worth it. The good news is that unlike an earthly contractor, He is always on call and always on time!

In our family, we love old TV shows. Some of our favorites are I Love Lucy, The Dick Van Dyke Show, The Andy Griffith Show, Hogan's Heroes and The Beverly Hillbillies. We've watched them so many times that there are many episodes in which we can quote the dialogue right along with the actors. We certainly know the words to all the theme songs. For that reason, I like to use the opening song from The Beverly Hillbillies to journal about the power of the Holy Spirit. If you don't know the words, they go like this:

My Journaling

Come and listen to my story about a man named Jed
A poor mountaineer, barely kept his family fed,
And then one day he was shootin' at some food,
And up through the ground come a bubblin' crude.

Oil that is, black gold, Texas tea[1].

One of the things that always fascinated me about the Clampets was that until Uncle Jed's shot went wide, they were incredibly poor. The very thing that would make them rich was always residing there just below the surface of their land . . . they just didn't know it!

My experience with the Holy Spirit is very similar. For too many years, I really felt powerless to make the changes in my life that God expected from me. I wanted to do better. To be

better. But no matter how hard I tried, I didn't seem to make significant progress. And then I learned what the problem was: I was trying to do the sanctification process by my own power. That just doesn't work. I needed help and the Helper I needed the most—the Holy Spirit—was always there ready and willing, I just didn't know it. I needed to find a way to appropriate the power of the Holy Spirit that was indwelling me and let

Him empower me to change what needed changing.

No drilling necessary, but we do need to plug in.

And while Uncle Jed found oil...you will find something much better. The Holy Spirit will be your Comforter, Guide and the best Source of wisdom you will ever find.

I can't close this chapter without touching on two benefits of allowing the Holy Spirit to have unfettered access to our lives, in my experience; these have added a richness to life that I want for everyone whom I love as well. In Romans, Paul spoke a blessing over the church when he said, "May the God of hope fill you with all joy and peace as you trust in him, so that you may overflow with hope by the power of the Holy Spirit." [2]

Isn't that just the most wonderful prayer to pray over the people whom you love? I think so—and I add it into almost every Legacy Journaling project I work on. The Holy Spirit brings joy and peace to our lives—two things in short supply in our day-to-day world. Joy is so different from happiness. It is not based on our circumstances at all. Joy springs from the hope that the Holy Spirit provides which supersedes anything going on in the world around us. This gives us peace that equips us to walk through whatever life brings with confidence and assurance.

The knowledge that the Holy Spirit of God has taken up residence in our lives, that He performs all these miraculous functions, that He dwells with us forever, and that He will never leave or forsake us is cause for great joy and comfort.

Thank God for this precious gift: the Holy Spirit and His work in our lives!

Who Am I Working On All Of These Legacy Journaling Projects For?

Inevitably, when I am teaching about **Stones of Remembrance** I have a student ask, just how many of these *Legacy Bibles* have you done? That's a fair question. I know that I have mentioned throughout this book several different recipients of *Legacy Bibles* that I have been working on while writing . . . so you may have the same question. This list is meant to both answer that question and perhaps prompt you with ideas of *Legacy Journaling* projects you may want to do yourself.

1. Family Legacy Bible (our personal family)
2. Family Legacy Bibles for three extended family members. These projects I have only begun and then gifted to the family for them to carry on. Sometimes just having a Bible that is not *blank* makes it easier for someone else to carry on with for themselves.
3. My son.
4. My nieces and nephew
5. Several new brides. I give the bride a wide-margin Bible with one or two entries in them to get them started. I have also been asked to create a new *Legacy Bible* as a guest book at a wedding. Each guest writes a note or prayer for the to the new couple beside their favorite verse and signs their name.

6. Several new Moms. This is my favorite baby shower gift to give these days. I have also done several starter *Legacy Bibles* to be given to the Mom and Dad the day they have their baby dedicated at church.
7. Family Reunion Bible—we've used a wide margin Bible to have everyone in attendance highlight their favorite verse and write a brief note in the margin and sign their name.
8. Graduation gifts. Even if you haven't already begun a Legacy Bible for someone in your family, a great time to start is at their graduation party. Let all the guests write a prayer or highlight a verse of encouragement and sign it and give it to the graduate.
9. While I do not yet have grandchildren, I will most certainly begin one for each grandchild I have.

Creative Walk Through Of My Entries

Contractor—1 Corinthians 6:19

The analogy that I used in my journaling was the inspiration for the imagery. I wanted to create the feel of a blueprint. I traced the floor plan (from the ***Stones of Remembrance One and Dones***) onto my page. Use a light hand to make the transfer so that you do not have to deal with dark lines you will need to erase later. I then painted several thin layers of watercolor over the whole page . . . and onto the piece of watercolor paper that I would use for the *tip-in* always drying each layer before adding more color. I've found this is the best way to build up more color rather than trying to accomplish it all at once. Let it dry completely. I then used my white gel pen to go over all of the lines to create the look of the blueprint.

To create a place for my journaling, I used a cardstock *tip-in* and used an architectural font to write the words *Holy Spirit*. I attached my journaling to the back of the card and added the card to the edge of the page.

Power Source—2 Corinthians 13:14

I'm going to keep it real with you. This entry has been a work in progress over several projects. The entry you see here is my THIRD pass at this. Now, let me say that the other two are still in existence and are actually in real live projects, but I was never thrilled with them, even though I made them work. I finally landed on an entry that I feel serves my purposes well, but it took some work that I will explain in just a moment.

Before I do, this is a great opportunity to share a couple of thoughts I have on the practicalities of creating *Legacy Journaling* entries. The first is that I do reuse illustrations across different journaling projects. I have several projects in the works and when I find an illustration that I think communicates what I want, I don't hesitate to use it again. If I do one that doesn't quite nail it, then I have another opportunity to find something that will work better the next time. The second is, as I've said before, not every entry is going to be stellar . . . we have to remember that *Legacy Journaling **is more about our heart than the art!*** We can't get too wrapped up worrying that our artwork isn't perfect. I guess what I am saying is to be kind to yourself, do your best and be more concerned with communicating your heart than the perfection of your art.

Let me walk you through the progression of how I landed on the current entry. The first illustration I did had a very elaborate oil derrick traced into the margin and was a LOT of work. Honestly, I didn't love it because it was too fussy without having a strong visual impact or connection to my journaling.

I went a totally different direction on the next one by incorporating **The Beverly Hillbillies** opening title graphic. But again, the end result was not my favorite. When I asked myself what I didn't like about it, the answer was that it put the attention on the wrong part of the story. This wasn't about **The Beverly Hillbillies**—it was about the **Holy Spirit**. I was only using Uncle Jed because it was a common experience that I had with the recipient of the Bible. I could still use it, but I didn't want it to be the focus.

When I realized I was trying to make too much of a connection with the oil that Uncle Jed found, it became clear that what I really wanted to communicate was the fact that we need to plug into the power of the Holy Spirit. I had my solution. I went back and changed my journaling just a bit to put more emphasis on the Holy Spirit being an abundant and available power supply that we can plug into. After this, I actually liked the journaling better too. So I knew that I could use a simple power plug to illustrate it—and I am much more satisfied with the entry over all. And may I say, it doesn't hurt to ask the Holy Spirit to give you inspiration to communicate what is in your heart.

May Hope Abound—Romans 15:13

I wanted to handwrite this verse as a prayer, so I created a very simple *tip-in* by stamping a frame of flowers[3] and then used watercolors to color it in. I stamped a few gold dots around the edges of the floral spray to add a bit of shine I then hand lettered the words "May Hope Abound" into the frame. I did a very light watercolor wash over the remainder of the page to help the simple card to stand out. The final touch was to add just a few of the stamped gold dots over the background just to tie the two together. I really like the simplicity of it. I added my journaling onto the back of the card and used washi tape to add the card to the page.

Inspiration

Holy Spirit Verses:

Psalm 51:11, Matthew 1:8, Matthew 3:11, Matthew 28:19, Mark 1:8, Mark 13:11, Luke 1:35, Luke 3:16, Luke 3:22, Luke 4:1, Luke 11:13, Luke 12:12, John 14:26, John 15:26, John 20:22, Acts 1:5, Acts 1:8, Acts 2:4, Acts 2:33, Acts 2:38, Acts 4:31, Acts 7:55, Acts 9:31, Acts 11:24, Acts 15:8, Romans 5:5, Romans 14:17, Romans 15:13, Romans 15:16, 1 Corinthians 6:19, 1 Corinthians 12, 1 Corinthians 14:1, 2 Corinthians 13:14, Galatians 5:22-23, Ephesians 1:13, Ephesians 4:30, 1 Thessalonians 1:5-6, 2 Timothy 1:14, Titus 3:5, Hebrews 2:4,

Holy Spirit Prompts:

1. Journal the Fruits of the Spirit found in Galatians 5:22-23.
2. Journal about the spiritual gifts that the Holy Spirit gives to each of us. If you know what your particular

gifts are, share those and how you have used them to encourage other Christ followers. (1 Corinthians 12-14)

3. If your project is a family Legacy Bible, consider journaling about various people in your family, the gifts they had, and how they used them throughout their lives.

Notes

[1] http://www.lyricsondemand.com/tvthemes/beverlyhillbillieslyrics.html
[2] Romans 15:13, New International Version, Thomas Nelson Publishers
[3] Floral stamp is by ALTENEW called Recollections. Released 2017

CHAPTER 12

The Stone of Wisdom

The fear of the Lord is the beginning of wisdom.
Proverbs 9:10

If any of you lacks wisdom, let him ask God
and He will give it to you.
James 1:5

In one of my personal journals, I found this note: "Knowledge is knowing the right thing to do; wisdom is actually doing it." In the margin, I had written this:

Formula for Wisdom
Wisdom = knowledge + obedience

I'm sure that my notes were my reflections on a sermon or a book I was reading at the time, and while I am not clear on the origins, I do know that since that time these thoughts have heavily influenced my understanding of wisdom. In a way, I think that an understandable definition of wisdom is applied knowledge. It is not only knowing what to do; it is also knowing when to do it and then following through to do it.

In our family, we use a term called possum thinking. If you haven't ever been around possums, they may not look pretty, but they can think of more ways to come at a problem than you might imagine. You probably know that a possum will play "dead" when a predator comes close wanting to make a tasty meal. Most animals don't want to eat dead meat they haven't killed themselves, so when they come upon a "dead" possum, they just keep on trucking. When they are gone, the possum comes back to life and goes on its merry way. We use the term possum thinking to encourage creative problem solving—applying knowledge to the problem in the right way to come up with the best resolution . . . wisdom, if you will.

When Weston was small, Royce would send him on little tasks around the house that he knew would provide opportunities for him to figure out himself ways to accomplish them. As his little brain would go to work, you could almost see the

wheels turning. Once when Royce was mowing the yard on the riding mower, he asked five-year old Weston to please pick up all the sticks in the yard so that he wouldn't run over them and hurt the mower. There were a LOT of sticks, but that didn't stop Weston from getting to work. He carried an armful of sticks at a time all the way around to the backyard where the burn pile was located. He had been working hard for just a little while when Royce realized that he hadn't seen him for a few minutes. He was about to go see what had distracted him from his task when Weston came around the corner of the house pulling his Red Rider wagon, which he began filling with piles of sticks rather than making a hundred trips to the burn pile. Royce gave him a wave and a *"there you go, son . . . that's possum thinking!"*

Over time, Royce no longer had to pose opportunities for Weston to practice possum thinking; as he handled everyday life, he just began to do it instinctively. A few years ago, Royce shattered his ankle and had to have it reconstructed. All in all, he was in a cast for several months, which limited his mobility. You don't have to be around Royce for very long to notice a couple of things about him: he will do anything he can to help you, but it isn't easy for him to ask for help. While he was healing from his injury, several of his normal daily "rituals" just weren't possible for him to accomplish. I returned from a business trip to find that a paracord attached to the blinds and strung across the bed, being looped around the bedpost. Apparently, Weston had noticed that his Dad wasn't able to get to the blinds with his cast on and knowing how much of a daily ritual it was for him to open the blinds first thing in the morning, he solved the problem. I loved it! He was taking knowledge and applying it to a problem out of love for his Dad. It wasn't pretty, but it was the heart and soul of possum thinking!

I want to communicate in my *Legacy Journaling* that as a family, we want to all become possum thinkers—applying God's truth to the situation at hand and acting upon it in the way He has instructed us to in His Word.

The best place to start is hiding as much of His Word as we can in our hearts so that we have it to draw upon when we need it. Yes, as James tells us, if we lack wisdom, all we have to do is ask God for it and He will give it to us.[1] But how much easier would life be if we did our homework sooner than the hour before class begins.

Oh dear, did I just betray my professor roots? I think I did. I love college students. I have found them to be one of my greatest sources of inspiration because they challenge my brain to stay young and to continue learning new things. But without a doubt, they have also provided many moments of great amusement as well. Tests and term papers are the bane of a college student's existence—and I might add that they aren't that much fun for the professors either! Inevitably, as I am on my way to administer a test (a test they have known was coming from the first day of class, via their syllabus), I will see students in the hallway or the quad hunkering down over their textbook, cramming for the last eight minutes before the class begins. I kid you not—it is rare that one of them doesn't actually ask, "Ms. Gray, is chapter four going to be on our test?" I just keep walking, laughing on the inside because I know there are fourteen questions from chapter four.

And don't even get me started on the topic of term papers. There are some college students who think they are possum

thinkers, but they are not. Technology is a wonderful thing…on both sides of the desk. Students can do research online rather than inside a physical library, and professors have an app through which they can run each paper to see if and how much of it the student has plagiarized. It takes three seconds, maybe less. It's a wonderful tool, but most of the time, I don't even need to use it. My precious, plagiarizing students (most students do not, by the way) often haven't even bothered to format the chunks of text that they've copied and pasted from an online article to match the font in their paper. They think they are being so smart, but in fact, they really are not . . . not by a country mile. You can see how this can make me giggle, right?

My application of this to my spiritual life is that I want to do the work that will prepare my heart for whatever life brings my way. If I find myself in a tough situation and have to do a quick search in order to know what wisdom needs to be applied, the likelihood is much greater that I won't find the best solution—or, heaven-forbid, apply it in the wrong way.

I use these examples in my *Legacy Journaling* because possum thinking is a family term and everyone knows I have been a college professor, so these are ways of uniquely applying this stone to our family experience. You will probably have similar types of stories to share from your family as well.

One note, I think humor is absolutely more-than-okay to use in your journaling. We are a family who loves to laugh. We love to play practical jokes on each other and we find humor in everyday life. If humor were absent on the pages of my *Legacy Journaling* entries, then it would not be a true reflection of who we are. Yes, God's Word is a serious thing and I don't mean to make light of it, but since He gave us a sense of humor, I think it is okay for us to use it as we share our encounters with God on the pages of His Word.

Finally, I am a huge fan of journaling through Proverbs. The entire book is chocked full of wisdom for everyday living. As a young girl, one of my Sunday School teachers pointed out that there are 31 Chapters in the Book of Proverbs. She said that this meant that we could read one chapter each day of the month, which became a personal habit of mine that I continue to this day.

A proverb that I try to use in all of my *Legacy Journaling* projects is Proverbs 21:21, *"Whoever pursues righteousness and unfailing love will find life, righteousness and honor."* These are usually quick entries based on my personal Bible journaling. I typically use a small decorative element, but keep the focus on the verse itself. I may add a note on the back of the small card about my personal encounter with these types of verses. Even though the entry is small, I like keeping the margin available for use by the recipient. I'm hopeful that it will encourage them to pick up a pen and add their own thoughts on the subject.

Creative Walk Through Of My Entries

Possum Thinking—Psalm 128

This is a short Psalm and it speaks to the joyfulness of those who fear the Lord and who follow Him in all their ways. It also says that our children will be like vigorous olive trees as they sit around our tables. All in all, it is a perfect picture of the benefits of applying God's Word and instructions to our lives. I have just taken our family's term, possum thinking, and given it a little twist so that it includes using God's Word to solve our every day problems.

To create this entry, I began by using a pencil to lightly outline the outside of the whole chapter. Then I did a light watercolor wash everywhere, except inside the pencil marks. I used a colored pencil in a darker shade than the background to cover over the pencil lines and draw a bit more attention to the highlighted verse. I also used a light gray marker to add a drop shadow on the top and left edges of the outlined box. If you like, for a variation you can add some doodling around the edges to form a bit of a frame and draw a bit more attention to the passage of scripture.

I then took a watercolor paper tip-in card and stamped the red wagon, along with some grass and a few sticks. This stamp is by Art Impression™ and is designed for you to put things into it, so I just sketched in the words POSSUM THINKING. I outlined the letters with my Micron and then added a little watercolor to the whole illustration. I then added just a bit of a gray watercolor wash around those letters to make them pop. My journaling was done on the backside of the card before I put it onto the edge of the page.

Let's Do Our Homework—James 1:5

This was an entry that I was able to create fairly quickly. I printed off my journaling (I typically type out this kind of journaling because it takes up less space than handwritten journaling) and determined how big a card I would need to create to contain the journaling. When I use printed journaling, I always sign and date the entry to give it a personal touch.

I used watercolor paper to create the *tip-in*. I used a Tim Holtz stamp of the stack of books and used watercolor paint to color the image. I added the title with hand lettering.

I added a watercolor wash to the Bible page and a few splatters just to give the page a bit of visual texture.

Alternate Background: Scrape brightly colored acrylic paint all over the page, except where you have highlighted the verse. Test this on a page in the back of the Bible first. It is possible to read through acrylic paint if you scrape it very thinly. You can use an old gift card or palette knife to scrape the paint onto the page in a very thin layer. Refer to the list of suggested supplies to make sure you are using an acrylic paint that will work well in your Bible.

Prouerbs 21:21

I love these little watercolor-stamping illustrations that are made with Art Impression™ stamps[2]. Once you learn a few simple techniques, you can create these little illustrations with just a few little stamps. Each one is different and unique. I have used them over and over again for most of my journaling entries in Proverbs. They are simple to create and they lend continuity to these similar types of entries. Check out the *Techniques* section of your workbook and the *Illuminated Journaling YouTube Channel* for instruction on creating your own watercolor illustrations.

You can have several of them done ahead of time and just select one to add to a page like this. If you are a crafter and have other supplies available to you, try creating a little visual interest for these cards by die-cutting shapes to do your stamping on. It is fun to find new uses for supplies we use in our other crafts.

Inspiration

Wisdom Verses:

Genesis 3:6, Exodus 31:3, Deuteronomy 1:13, Deuteronomy 4:6, 1 Kings 3:10, 1 Kings 10:7, 1 Chronicles 22:12, 2 Chronicles 1:10, Job 12:13, Job 28:17, Psalm 90:12, Psalm 111:10, All of Proverbs, Proverbs 9:10 Ecclesiastes 2:13,

Isaiah 33:6, Jeremiah 9:23, Daniel 2:3, Matthew 13:54, Luke 2:52, Luke 7:35, Romans 11:33, 1 Corinthians 1:24, 1 Corinthians 2:1-5, 1 Corinthians 3:19, Ephesians 1:8, Ephesians 1:17, Colossians 1:9, Colossians 2:3, Colossians 3:16, James 1:5, James 3:13, James 3:17, Revelations 5:12

Wisdom Prompts:

1. If you are working on a project for child that is growing up, consider using the Bible story of the Queen of Sheba and Solomon to illustrate Wisdom. (1 Kings 10:7)
2. Consider taking the life of Daniel and sharing how he exhibited wisdom throughout his life, even in difficult situations. (Daniel 1:3-21)
3. Create an entry in Ecclesiastes 2:13: "Wisdom is better than foolishness, just as light is better than darkness." Use a light bulb and let it dispel the darkness to the edges of the page.
4. Journal your way through Proverbs and invite family members to write a note next to their favorite proverb, sharing why it has changed their life.
5. Write a prayer asking God to give wisdom to the recipient of the Legacy Bible. Two verses that work well for this are Ephesians 1:17 and Colossians 1:9.

Notes

1 James 1:5 New International Version, Thomas Nelson Publishers
2 Art Impressions has a line of products specifically designed to make creating small watercolor paintings easy for any skill level of artist.

CHAPTER 13

The Stone of Obedience

To obey is better than sacrifice.
2 Samuel 15:22

The law of the Lord is perfect,
refreshing the soul.
The statutes of the Lord are trustworthy,
making wise the simple.
The precepts of the Lord are right,
giving joy to the heart.
The commands of the Lord are radiant,
giving light to the eyes.
The fear of the Lord is pure,
enduring forever.
The decrees of the Lord are firm,
and all of them are righteous.
They are more precious than gold,
than much pure gold;
they are sweeter than honey,
than honey from the honeycomb.
By them your servant is warned;
in keeping them there is great reward.
Psalm 19:7-11

Can we just camp out a minute together and look a bit deeper into this passage in Psalm 19? If someone were to just ask me what I thought about obedience, I would not naturally use the words that are put together in the same sentences in this passage. The law is refreshing? The commands of the Lord are radiant, giving light to the eyes? The decrees of the Lord are sweeter than honey?

If I am being authentic with you and with myself, being obedient isn't one of my strong suits. Being strong willed? Stubborn? Independent? Yes—those are the things that come way more naturally to me. Even so, I don't want to miss out on the blessings of God out of stubbornness or thick-headedness!

You already know that my grandmother, Jammy Jane, is one of my spiritual heroes. I want to be like her when I grow up. And I certainly never wanted to disappoint her when I was a child. When it comes to height, I've always been on the short side. One Sunday when we went to church during a summer visit, there was a very tall man sitting right in front of us, blocking my view. It wasn't like I could move to the right or the left to see any better because beside him was his tall wife wearing a hat and their three boys . . . who were also gi-ants. So I improvised . . . I just stood up so I could see.

I felt Jammy Jane's hand tug on my skirt. Of course, I knew she wanted me to sit down, but I kept standing because there was something interesting going on in the pulpit. Final-ly, she leaned forward and whispered, "I need you to sit down" . . . which I did, but I wasn't happy about it. As we were walking out of church, she complimented me on being obedient. But before she had even taken a breath, I informed her, "Well, I did sit down, but I was standing up on the in-side!" [Have I mentioned that I am honest to a fault?] To which she laughed and said, "Well that's a start! Now we just have to work on the inside."

I have come to truly believe that obedience originating from the inside out is what these verses are referring to, not the mere appearance of obedience. Obedience isn't easy. Our nature is to want to do what we want to do when we want to do it. Obedience is an act of our will—an act that first requires that we know what is required so we can do it. I once had a pastor share that delayed obedience isn't obedience at all. It has much of the same attitude attached to it that my "I was standing up on the inside" speech had: willfulness.

I am strong-willed and some might say that because of that, I don't have as much authority to speak on the subject of obedience. But I disagree. Our authority doesn't come from our ability to do right, but from God's ability to enable us to do what is right. None of my success in any area of my life comes from my own strength or goodness, so the fact that this area is more difficult for me speaks to God's grace and mercy when He enables me to succeed.

I am a living and breathing billboard for Ezekiel 36: 26. I can speak to the power of God to remove my stubborn heart of stone and replace it with a tender and responsive heart of flesh. I obey Him because I love Him, because it benefits me and because following His statutes helps me be an honorable ambassador for Him here on earth. The fact that I didn't come into this world as a naturally obedient person [not one of us ever really has] provides me an excellent opportunity to share a personal testimony in my Legacy Journaling projects. We don't want to avoid sharing the parts of our faith that are difficult—rather, this is a place that we ought to share with as much authenticity as we can. Here is an example of how I share.

My Journaling

I came into this world with an opinion…about e-v-e-r-y-t-h-i-n-g. And to make it worse, I think I'm right most of the time. That is not a pretty combination in a 2 year old or a 52 year old. As I was growing up, this also got in the way of having the kind of intimate relationship with the Lord that I wanted. When you think your opinions are *"all that and a bag of chips,"* you tend to expect an explanation before you decide whether you will be obedient or not. If I asked my parents "why" once, I bet I asked them a thousand times just in the first few months after my adoption [I was two when they adopted me]. It is a wonder they kept me! And I have certainly hounded God with that same three-letter word over the course of our relationship. But here is what I've come to realize: *asking why I should do something is based on a false assumption . . . the assumption that I am the best person to judge what is good for me—and I'm not!*

There I said it. I will never have the mind of God. My opinions are neither all that, nor are they a bag of chips! These verses in Psalm 19 tell me why I need to give up doing things my way and get on with letting God's Word inform my behavior and choices. As someone a bit further down the path, I can honestly say that the rewards of obedience are better than it has ever felt to be stubborn and do things my own way. If you want to know what happened to change my heart, flip over to Ezekiel 36.

I love being able to connect scriptures together because this gives context to the subject at hand. And since obedience, at least for me, is a very complex subject, I try to share about it from a couple of different angles. Here is my journaling for the Ezekiel passage.

My Journaling

I hate to admit the number of times that my stubbornly strong will has gotten me into a heap of trouble, but it has...a lot. And as good as digging your heals into the ground and refusing to budge may feel in the moment, it feels equally bad afterwards. Ask me how I know. I hate having to retrace my steps to the place where I went astray and I hate apologizing. But I have a lot of practice at both. It stinks.

In the aftermath of a particularly awful decision, I asked God why I was so stupid and stubborn . . . and he had a particularly interesting insight—the problem wasn't my stubbornness, it was my heart. Mark tells us that *"It is what comes from inside that defiles you. For from within, out of a person's heart, come evil thoughts, sexual immorality, theft, murder, adultery, greed, wickedness, deceit, lustful desires, envy, slander, pride, and foolishness."*[1] Yep, that pretty much nails it!

So, if the problem is my heart, what can I do about it? I love this passage in Ezekiel because God has a solution for Israel's heart problem and He has one for me too. Read the part that I have highlighted.[2] This is such a perfect description of what both the problem and solution has been for me: my heart of stone needed to be replaced by a heart of flesh. I knew the problems my stone heart had gotten me into, so I was ready to trade up! I have never regretted

it. Now I am stubborn about keeping the commands of the Lord and they never lead me down the wrong path or require me to make an apology.

Here is the passage I have highlighted, *"Then I will sprinkle clean water on you, and you will be clean. Your filth will be washed away, and you will no longer worship idols. And I will give you a new heart, and I will put a new spirit in you. I will take out your stony, stubborn heart and give you a tender, responsive heart. And I will put my Spirit in you so that you will follow my decrees and be careful to obey my regulations."*

So many times in scripture we are given a promise that is conditional based upon our obedience. One of those times is found in Joshua 1:8. *Keep this Book of the Law always on your lips; meditate on it day and night, so that you may be careful to do everything written in it. Then you will be prosperous and successful.*

Our obedience isn't to a contrary God. His instructions are for our benefit…and there are definitely rewards for keeping His commandments that far exceed keeping us from having to apologize. Creating entries in our *Legacy Journaling* projects can help our readers discover those rewards and benefits for themselves—and perhaps not have to learn this particular lesson the hard way.

Creative Walk Through Of My Entries

Bag of Chips—Psalm 19

It's okay to let your personality and sense of humor show. When we show that we can laugh at ourselves, it allows others to laugh along with us. It also keeps us connected. I simply couldn't help myself. I always start out by writing my journaling—it can then guide what I choose to illustrate, letting me know how much room I need to save.[3] Because this journaling was longer, I knew that I was going to have to have a tip-in to allow for all the extra words. And, as hard as I tried finding the imagery from the scripture passage, (yes, I thought about using dripping honey and piles of gold) I just couldn't get away from the bag of chips that was in the forefront of my brain. So I went with it.

A quick Google search gave me lots of chip options, so I found one that I could easily recreate. I resized it and printed it out. I traced it into my Bible, knowing that the tip-in was going to cover it up a bit. So I made sure that enough of the image would show to the viewer before they lifted the flap. I also chose to rewrite a portion of the scripture passage on the tip-in rather than continuing the illustration onto the card as I have done on other entries. There are no rules so let each entry speak what works best to communicate to the reader.

Because this is a two-part entry, with the second passage being in Ezekiel 36, I chose to not only give the reference, but also to provide the page so the viewer would have an easy time finding the second entry.

I completed the illustration with my regular process of blocking in the color with watercolors and then adding detail and shading with colored pencils.

Heart of Stone—Ezekiel 36

It is crazy what you will find if you do a Google search for heart of stone. To save you the grief, I have included the image I used for this entry in the **Stones of Remembrance One and Dones**.

I had intended to add the complete illustration to the Bible page—and I think that would have worked quite well too. But I wanted to emphasize the change that happens when God replaced my heart of stone with a heart of flesh. So I chose to trace the stone heart portion of the illustration onto a piece of heavy vellum and trace the heart of flesh portion directly onto the bible page. I intentionally left the vellum page large so that I could match the two illustrations up when I attached the vellum to the page. I then colored both illustrations with colored pencils. I added the two titles to the individual parts of this illustration. I wanted something that would visually tie the two illustrations together so I chose to add some gold foil squares and a bit of gold stamping to both pages. If you would like more instruction on adding foil to a Bible page, please refer to the *Techniques* section of your workbook.

Once all the pieces were complete, I put the vellum piece on top of the heart illustration and marked where I would need to trim the page so that they would line up. I cut the vellum to size and attached it with double sided tape to the inside edge of the page.

Note: If you want to create something similar using the art that is provided in the **Stones of Remembrance One and Dones**, I realize that the "*heart of flesh*" is only partially visible in the illustration. I simply traced the parts that were visible and then used a pencil to fill in the remaining outline. Don't let this part stress you out. You will notice that my finished heart isn't exactly perfect—which is fitting because my real heart is still far from perfect as well!

Inspiration

Obedience Verses:

Leviticus 18:4, Deuteronomy 6:3, Deuteronomy 6:24, Deuteronomy 7:9, Deuteronomy 13:4 Deuteronomy 30:14, 1 Samuel 15:22, Psalm 19:7-11, Psalm 40:8, Psalm 69:5-6, Psalm 86:11-12, Psalm 94:12, Psalm 119:18, Proverbs 12:1, Proverbs 15:32, Isaiah 38:16,Ezekiel 36:26-27, Mark 7:20-22, Acts 5:29, Galatians 6:3, Philippians 2:12, Hebrews 12:5

Obedience Prompts:

1. Personal testimonies are great for this topic. Experience speaks volumes, so share what you have learned. You don't have to share the gory details—that isn't always necessary. But do share enough that the reader knows why you have come to your conclusions.
2. Choose a few of these verses and just rewrite them in the margins. Do some stamping or doodles around them and create a colorful background. Let the words speak for themselves.
3. If you are doing this for a child, it might be fun to record some of their funny "misbehaviors" near some of the verses on obedience. This lighthearted memory can underscore that we come into this world with a sinful

nature—and the fact that they still have to battle with it as adults is just part of the ongoing sanctification process.

Notes

[1] Mark 7:20-22, New Living Translation, Tyndale House Publishers
[2] Ezekiel 36:25-27 New Living Translation, Tyndale House Publishers
[3] For more tips on journaling, check out the *Journaling Tips and Tricks* section in your workbook.

CHAPTER 14

The Stone of Gratitude

Give thanks to the Lord for He is good.
Psalm 118:1

Give thanks in all circumstances;
for this is God's will for you in Christ Jesus.
1 Thessalonians 5:18

When upon life's billows you are tempest tossed,
When you are discouraged, thinking all is lost,
Count your many blessings; name them one by one,
And it will surprise you what the Lord has done.[1]

One of the first things we learn as children is to count. It's an essential. As we learn to count, we learn that we can keep track of things. We are "counting people"…it's almost like we can't help ourselves. We ask a child, "How old are you?" and even the very young will hold up the correct number of fingers. All the developmental toys help children learn to count.

Counting is something that I have learned is fundamental to being a Christ follower too. Learning to count our blessings when times are good is essential because there will come a day when times are difficult that we will need to fall back on that basic skill. When you follow Christ and you stop counting your blessings, it is a bit like running around in the forest, on the edge of a cliff, in the dark, without a flashlight . . . do it long enough and you will eventually fall off!

There is hope and transformative power in counting our blessings and naming the good gifts of God. If we begin to see all of our blessings piled up in one place, then we will realize that God has been acting on our behalf in a mighty way—and we can believe that He will do so again.

There is a difference between having a heart filled with gratitude and engaging in praise and worship, which is why I have dedicated separate stones for each of them. Gratitude is about reflecting on the personal encounters we have with God and how he has taken care of us. It is being thankful for those blessings and seeing his hand in our everyday interactions with him. Praise and Worship acknowledges who he is—it is our gift back to him. Of course there is an overlap because we can't help but praise him when our heart is filled with gratitude!

A   **B**
Adoption   Bible
Anastasia   Bills Paid

C   **D**
Camp   Dance Recital
Choir Tour

E   **F**
End of School   Family
    Friends

G   **H**
Guatemala   Healing/Back
Adoption   Home
Agency

My Journaling

As a children's Sunday School teacher, one year we took a different letter of the alphabet each week and we wrote down all of our blessings that began with that letter. It changed this teacher's perspective. Kids are much better counters than we are as adults and I decided back then to dust off my counting skills and be intentional about counting my blessings. I started keeping a composition book with different letters written every couple of pages—I call it my *Blessings Account Book.*

Over the years, I have added entries under those letters of the blessings and now, because I am old, I have a book filled with all the wonderful things that God has done for me. When times are hard and I am not feeling all that thankful, I go to that book and it changes my perspective very quickly. It moves my heart from grumbling to being able to truly give thanks to the Lord . . . for He is good and I do not forget his benefits.[2]

I want to share a few of my favorites with you—and you will notice I've left room for you to add your own. You may even need to start your own *Blessings Account Book* . . . I'm just sayin'.

Creative Walk Through Of My Entries

Count Your Blessings – Psalms 118:1

Count Your Blessings is an invitation to the young lady that was the recipient of this *Legacy Journaling Bible* not only to see what *I* count as blessings, but also to begin to add her own blessings to this list. I specifically included things that she was familiar with to encourage her to see where our blessings overlap and where we have shared experiences. I added items to the list that were things I counted as blessings because they had happened in her life and I was grateful for that. I also used language that is common between us—she is forever ending conversations with, "I'm just sayin'," so I couldn't resist ending my note to her with her favorite phrase.

Our gratitude doesn't need to be focused solely on ourselves and this was a way to model that through the entry. Because this gift has already been given to a real person, I am so overjoyed to be able to share with you that she has since added to it—and that she was anxious to show me her list the last time we were together. I had to go add that experience into my own *Blessings Account Book*...I couldn't have been more pleased! Because this was mostly about the list, I wanted to keep the imagery focused on counting our blessings and also make it easy for her to add her own journaling to the page if she wanted to.

I had a piece of acetate that had gold numbers printed on it that I decided to use as the base of my *tip-in*. I cut two matching pieces of white cardstock to make the cover and to place on the other side of the acetate to cover up the adhesive. I stamped *Count Your Blessings* on the front card using a stamp set called Botanical Letters by Papertrey Ink.[3] I then attached the list of blessing on the piece of cardstock on the back. I did a quick watercolor wash of yellows and golds to give the *tip-in* a nice background to rest on.

I Always Thank God For You -- 1 Corinthians 1:4

Another way that I address gratitude in *Legacy Journaling* is simply to tell the recipient of the Bible what I am grateful for about them. *I Always Thank God For You* is a simple en-

try. I hand-lettered the title on 1
Corinthians 1:4 *I always thank my*
God for you because of his grace
given you in Christ Jesus—and
then I wrote a brief letter about
how grateful I am to have her in
my life. I have learned so much
from her because she has modeled
having a heart filled with gratitude
from the moment I first met her.
Because of this, she has had an impact on my personal relationship

with Jesus. *Legacy Journaling* isn't always about passing on
our own insight and wisdom, but it can also be a great way to
share how the family as a whole has influenced one another.
Our individual gifts can build one another up and help us
more deeply love the Lord. This isn't the only entry of this
type that I have done. I always try to add a letter to the recipient that is meant to share my gratitude for them in my life and
how they have influenced me. This type of entry could be
used under any of the various stone topics.

Inspiration

Gratitude Verses:

1 Chronicles 16:34, 1 Chronicles 29:13, Psalm 7:17, Psalm
9:1, Psalm 103:2, Psalm 107:15, Psalm 118:1, Isaiah 25:1,
Jeremiah 33:11, Matthew 15:36 (Jesus gave thanks), 1 Corinthians 1:4, Philippians 1:3, Colossians 3:16, 1 Thessalonians
5:18

Gratitude Prompts:

1. Create your own list of counted blessings.

2. Create a scavenger hunt of your favorite verses about being thankful or grateful. Begin with a verse like Psalms 118:1 and then give the reference to the next scripture at the bottom of that page. Leave notes of encouragement when you have applied this to your own walk with the Lord.

3. Create an envelope with strips of paper in it, some of which are filled out with your own blessings, but also with blanks available for others to add to it as they read what you have written.

4. At a family reunion or a Thanksgiving dinner, have everyone in attendance fill out a card with what they are thankful for and share them around the table. Let everyone know that you are going to collect them and add them into the family Legacy Bible. This may even become a family tradition. How cool would it be to have a collection of several years' lists of how God has blessed your family.

5. Write a letter each year to the recipient telling them what you are most grateful for in their life and how you have seen God protect and bless them that year. You can pick a different verse about being thankful or you can just keep adding to your previous notes, letting them build up in a pile on the page. This is especially great if you are creating this *Legacy Bible* for a child who is growing up and will eventually leave home with it in hand as a testimony of God's faithfulness in their life.

Notes

[1] Count Your Blessings, hymn by Johnston Oatman Jr., 1897
[2] Psalm 103:2
[3] Papertrey Ink stamps are only available on their website:
www.papertreyink.com

Chapter 15

The Stone of Praise

*This is my God, and I will **praise** him!*
Exodus 15:2

He alone is your God, the only one who is worthy of your
***praise**, the one who has done these mighty miracles that you*
have seen with your own eyes.
Deuteronomy 10:21

*I will **praise** the Lord at all times.*
*I will constantly speak his **praises**.*
Psalm 34:1

I will bring honor to your name in every generation.
*Therefore, the nations will **praise** you forever and ever.*
Psalm 45:17

I chose the word praise for my stone, but you may also have included words like worship, offering and sacrifice. I have combined these options all together for this stone because they are very much a part of how we respond to God. In fact, I could have called this the stone of our response. Use whatever words feel right for you—again, this is just our framework, right?

Two of the things I strive to communicate about praise in my Legacy Journaling projects are that we will never run out of things to praise God for, and that we can praise Him with everything we do. I used to think that praising God happened only when I was singing praises to Him, but now I know that it really does go far beyond that. The Bible says that our lives are to be a sacrifice of praise.[1]

I have been blessed to have a personal relationship with Jesus for more than four decades (it makes me sound younger to use a single digit number), but there are things that I still have not yet even begun to grasp. This morning, I had breakfast with a delightful young lady. She actually came in to work on her day off just so we could talk. She works as a waitress at the state park where I have been on a writing retreat to finish up this book. and she has been an absolute joy every time I have sat in her section for lunch or dinner.

In one of our brief encounters over the menu, she shared that she had asked Jesus into her heart in the past couple of years. She was bubbling over with love and praise for Him. She asked if I would like to get together to have coffee sometime so that we could just talk, so we ended up meeting for breakfast. That is an hour that I will never forget. Her life hasn't always been easy. She said that some of the difficulties were because of her choices, while some were a result of simply being in the wrong place at the wrong time. Tears welled up in my eyes as she shared her testimony. My heart hurt for the pain that she has experienced and then it rejoiced with her as she turned from telling those difficult memories to telling me how she now knows that Jesus was with her every step of the way. She said, "Miss Jann, you know that you can run to the end of the earth, but Jesus is there. You can think you are totally alone, but you're not. Jesus is there—even if you think you want to be anywhere but where He is. And I can't stop praising Him for not abandoning me, when I wanted to abandon Him."

That is some powerful praise!

She then shared that when she realized what she had been running from was the only thing on earth worth running toward, she responded to Christ's invitation to let Him be her Lord and Savior. She said, "I've never looked back. I get up everyday and can't wait to see what kind of adventure Jesus and I are going to have today . . . and what new reasons I will have to praise Him!"

That expression of excitement and anticipation on her part caused me to have an "aha" moment of my own.

Her enthusiasm led me to realize that perhaps some of my praise has become too familiar. I thank God all the time for things I see in the world around me—and He certainly deserves praise for all this. I also praise Him for all that He has done, which is also absolutely deserved. I praise Him for who He is . . . sometimes to the point that it takes my breath away. But it is familiar praise. I believe I may have lost a bit of the wonder of anticipating with excitement what He will do next. Children and new believers don't approach God with familiar praise. Their praise is instinctive and unexpected because they are still surprised by the wonders that He does. I bet God's heart just fills up when they do this! He is always surprising me. He does things beyond what I can imagine or dream of, so I want to introduce that spontaneity back into my praise and worship of Him. I am grateful for the time with my new friend. She showed me another way to make my life a sacrifice of praise and that is a lesson I will take with me from this time forward.

In one of my *Legacy Journaling* projects, I have chosen several verses that focus on different aspects of our praise and worship. My illustrations focus on the unique characteristic of praise that the respective verse mentions. Although I have used different verses in my various projects, I have included Psalms 145:3 in all of them. *"Great is the Lord! He is most worthy of praise! No one can measure His greatness."* You can see from the illustration I chose to use that I went with a very literal interpretation of the scripture. The silliness of trying to measure God's greatness with a tape measure will not be lost on even the youngest child. Don't feel like every entry is in need of a huge explanation. Sometimes it is enough just to point out the verse and let it speak for itself.

One of the reasons that I have actually come to love using a bit of watercolor on most of my pages is that when I add water, it changes the texture and feel of the page. Yes, it does get a bit crinkly, but once the Bible is closed for a period of time, it really does smooth back out. It is the reaction between the water and the sizing [the chemical publishers use to help the page resist dirt and grime] that causes the page to feel different than it did before, even when it has flattened back out after I've finished working on it. As I flip through the pages of one of my journaling Bibles, my fingers sometimes know before my eyes do that I am coming to a page that contains journaling. This change can actually work in your favor when you give one of these *Legacy Bibles* as a gift. You don't have to do fancy entries on every single page. The recipient's fingers are going to know they are about to turn to something you wanted them to see…and that alone will keep them turning the pages.

My second example is another one I try to incorporate into most of my *Legacy Journaling* projects. It gives me the opportunity to explain a bit about Bible journaling and why it has become such an important part of my ongoing relationship with God. Remember, not everyone to whom you give a gift like this will be familiar with Bible journaling. Years from now, it may not even be a thing. I have chosen to give a bit of an explanation in the context of the *stone of praise.*

My journaling is an offering of praise to the Lord. It is only one way that I praise Him, but it is definitely an act of praise to Him. It is my way of saying, *"I read Your Word and I am consumed with love for You! Your Word has shown me something new about You that I didn't know before—and now I do…and I praise You for it!"*

When I sit down to work in my personal Bible, God already knows that this is my attitude, but because *Legacy Journaling* isn't just for an audience of One, I have felt the need to specifically address my purpose and intent for the wider audience that will eventually open up this Bible and see the work I have done there. I may no longer be around to give an explanation and I wouldn't want them to draw any conclusion other than that I did it to give honor and praise to my God and King!

Psalm 96:8-9 provides a great place for me to share my perspective on Bible Journaling. *"Give the Lord the glory he deserves! Bring your offering and come into his courts. Worship the Lord in all his holy splendor. Let the earth tremble before him."* I will usually

write this as a letter to the recipient. I want it to be a personal explanation to them, but I do keep in mind that in all likelihood, they will not be the only ones that read it. Here is a brief outline of what I usually share.

> *Dear* _____, *This Bible is a gift of love to you and to God. Even if you and I had the opportunity to spend hours and hours together talking about why we both love Jesus so much, we would never get to cover it all. I wanted you to have this Bible as a way to share with you the things that have had a life-changing impact on my relationship with Jesus, just in case we never get to talk about them all. And every time I have worked on the pages of this Bible, I have tried my best to make it a worthy offering of praise to God. He deserves all the honor and glory. You both have my heart! With Love, Jann*

It varies a bit, depending on the recipient of the gift, but you get the gist of what I try to communicate. I recognize that this Bible may take on a life of it's own—in fact, I pray that it will. That is why leaving at least a brief explanation of why I have spent the time creating what they see on these pages just makes sense to me. Think about that for your own projects and what you may want to express to both the recipient and others who will have the joy of looking at this legacy of love you have created.

Undoubtedly, this particular stone of remembrance is more of a boulder! I have only given you a smidgen of an idea of what is possible and I know your own creativity will suggest so much more as you begin to work on your own project. Just like the Stone of Gratitude, this topic allows you to get very personal in the things that you choose to journal about and highlight. Your family will have visual reflections that are your own unique reasons to praise and worship God. Journal those for sure! Your recipient will treasure these and be inspired to add their own.

Creative Walk Through Of My Entries

Beyond Measure—Psalm 145:3

I used the measuring tape found in the **Stones of Remembrance One and Dones** to trace the image into my Bible. I copied the image onto vellum and colored it and cut it out. I did a quick watercolor wash over the Bible page—leaving the verse free from paint.

To create the *tip-in*, I used a piece of watercolor paper and stamped the circle background stamp with embossing ink and applied white embossing powder. After melting the embossing powder with a heat tool, I used various colors of blue watercolor to fill in the open areas. Stickers were used to create the title and then the *tip-in* was added with washi tape.

Ascribe To The Lord—Psalm 96:8-9

I began by masking off the verses [for more instruction on masking, check out the Journaling Techniques section in your workbook]. Once the masking fluid was dry, I created a soft background with watercolor washes and some splatters. I used a watercolor *tip-in* card and did a small illustration at the bottom with watercolor stamping. I then wrote the focal verse above the illustration. I wrote my letter to the recipient on the back of the *tip-in* card before I added it to the page edge. It is just easier to do hand journaling before you attach it—and I wanted this note to be in my own handwriting, making it even a bit more personal.

Inspiration

Praise Verses:

Exodus 15:2, Deuteronomy 8:10, Deuteronomy 10:21, 2 Samuel 22:4, 2 Samuel 22:47, 1 Kings 8:56, 1 Chronicles 16:9, 1 Chronicles 16:25, 1 Chronicles 16:32, 1 Chronicles 29:13, Ezra 3:11, Job 1:21, Psalm 5:11, Psalm 7:17, Psalm 9:11, Psalm 26:12, Psalm 28:6, Psalm 31:21, Psalm 34:1, Psalm 35:10, Psalm 35:18, Psalm 42:11, Psalm 45:17, Psalm 48:10, Psalm 54:6, Psalm 66:20, Psalm 68:19, Psalm 69:34, Psalm 86:9, Psalm 96:2, Psalm 96:8-9, Psalm 98:7, Psalm 100:4, Psalm 106:1, Psalm 108:1, Psalm 145:3, Psalm 150, Isaiah 25:1, Mark 11:9, Luke 1:46, Luke 13:13, Ephesians 1:3, Ephesians 1:6, Hebrews 13:15, Jude 1:24

Praise Prompts

1. Share a story of a specific time when you were compelled to give praise to the Lord. Give specifics and share what sort of long-term impact it has had on your life.
2. If this Bible is for a child, create an entry that tells why you praise God for them.

3. Take the letters P-R-A-I-S-E and provide examples of reasons that you praise God that begin with each letter. You could do these all in one entry or create a bit of a scavenger hunt so you lead your viewer through several verses that illustrate these reasons one at a time.

4. Create a place for your recipient to write in the reasons they have to praise God.

5. Create a *Birthday Pocket of Praise* [you can find a template for this pocket in your workbook]. Trace (or draw your own) little pocket and adhere it to the margin of the Bible. Cut strips of paper and place them in the pocket, ready for you to add entries each year. This is a way to document significant reasons that you praised God in the year leading up to their birthday. Update it each year on their birthday. Be sure to add the date onto each strip when you make a new entry.

Notes

[1] Hebrews 13:15, New Living Translation, Tyndale House Publishers

CHAPTER 16

The Stone of Prayer

*Be joyful in hope, patient in affliction, faithful in **prayer**.*
Romans 12:12

My grandfather was a carpenter. The same summer I learned to iron with Jammy Jane, I learned to build things with Gramps. He was known for his cabinetry and furniture, but he could build a house from the ground up. That particular summer, he was working on a house he had purchased that was in very poor condition, but which he intended to turn into a wonderful home for some lucky family. In my book, Gramps was the original house *flipper*!

I loved the days when he would take me to work with him. He found overalls for me to wear that were just like his, along with a girl-sized hammer that fit perfectly into the loop on the side. My job was to pull the nails out of the boards that he was tearing out of the walls. Gramps reused wood and taught me to look at things that others would discard as having un-limited potential . . . if you could only just use your imagination. He taught me to *"measure twice and cut once, and if a thing is worth doing, it is worth doing well."* On more than one occasion, these life lessons have been so helpful.

And he taught me to pray.

Gramps was a whistler and he made up his own tunes. He whistled while he worked, while he walked, and while he drove. No need for a boom box or radio when Gramps was around—anything other than his whistle would have felt like noise. One day, I was busy pulling nails from the boards and he was staining a cabinet that he was about to install and just whistling away—and then he stopped and it was quiet. The silence was very noticeable after the lively tune he had been whistling. I kept waiting for him to start back up, but he didn't. Finally, I asked him why he stopped.

Gramps said, *"When I whistle, I talk with God, telling him all the things that are on my mind. When I stop, I'm listening. Prayer is a conversation with God—and it wouldn't be much of a conversation if I did all the talking."* So there it was: wisdom from a carpenter about talking to a Carpenter—he should know! Right there on that day, I began my own life-long habit of talking and listening to God, a practice that my relationship with God has benefited from more than anything else I have ever learned. God desires to speak into our lives. Yes, He wants to hear what is on my heart, but to change my heart, I need to spend time listening to what He says I need to do. I need to learn to recognize his voice in the midst of all the noise that surrounds me. I chose to use Proverbs 1:5 for my *Legacy Journaling* entry about Gramps' perspective on prayer, *"Let the wise hear...."*

Having regular conversations in times of prayer with God is an essential to the life of a follower of Christ. I wanted to reaffirm the power of prayer in my Legacy Journaling entries and had many, many stories that I could have shared to illustrate God's faithfulness in hearing and answering my prayers. I chose to share a story from one of my mission trips to Russia because it underscores that even when we only have a little faith to bring to the situation, God can outshine our limited supply and provide exceedingly and abundantly beyond what we can even ask for.

The focus of this trip to Russia was to take some of the most needed, but hard to get medicines to children's hospitals. We also wanted to host Christmas parties for the kids. The larger team of almost 600 people had started in Moscow, but then we took bus groups of 30 people out to smaller towns and villages where missions teams rarely went. I was a bus captain and I loved the opportunity to lead an amazing group of people who had the ability to love on children in ways I'd rarely seen before. I honestly felt like I was learning more from them than what I was providing to them as a leader, but I was soaking it up and loving every minute of it.

We arrived at a small children's hospital in Orel, Russia on a very cold winter's day. I never was good at converting Celsius to Fahrenheit, but my journal says that it was -22°C! Let's just say that it was crazy cold! As soon as our bus pulled up, there was a doctor and an administrator standing outside waiting for us (without coats, mind you.) As the bus captain, I would usually get off the bus and go inside to talk with the hospital administrator about how they wanted to proceed with the day, how they wanted us to deliver the medication and other details along those lines. But that day, the doctor and administrator walked to the bus and climbed onboard the moment we came to a stop.

We barely exchanged greetings before the doctor began speaking. He sounded very stern and I could tell by the expression on the face of my interpreter that what he was saying wasn't a normal explanation of the hospital and what our people would find when they came inside. He was speaking over the buses microphone, so when he finished and the interpreter began to share what the doctor had said, it too was spoken over the microphone so everyone on the bus could hear.

He said, *"We know that you are Christians and that you bring us medicine that we need very much . . . and we are grateful. But, if you are going to come in and tell our children, our families and our staff that they can trust God, we need you to prove that He is trustworthy to us before we will allow you to tell them something that would give them false hope. As you know, we have not been a country that has much use for God—and that may have been a mistake. We are willing to see if it were a mistake. We ask that you come and pray over a child that we have not been able to heal. She is dying. She will be dead by the end of the day if your God does not heal her. We think this is the way to see if what you say has merit."*

Oh my! My heart was beating out of my chest…and there was silence on the bus with everyone's eyes on me—

including the doctor's. I don't mind admitting that I was quickly asking God, *"What do you want me to do?"* And you might think that God spoke words of assurance and wisdom into my ear, but the only thing I heard was, *"Go pray!"*

So I looked the doctor in his eye and said, *"We will pray over this child."*

Walking into the hospital, my mind kept going to James 5:15 where the brother of Jesus tells us that if *"any of you are sick let them call for the elders of the church to come and pray over you . . .. Such a prayer offered in faith will heal the sick, and the Lord will make you well."* In truth, I didn't feel much like an elder of the church, but I also was more focused on the words, *"such a prayer offered in faith will heal the sick."*

It absolutely broke my heart to walk into the room where this child was receiving care. There were other children lying on other beds, accompanied by their parents and several caregivers. It struck me that should this child die, it would be in full view of the other children, no doubt causing them fear for their own lives. Never had I wanted to have the power to speak life and healing over someone's life than I did in that moment . . . and I knew that the only source of healing was going to be from God.

I asked my interpreter to translate for me and I asked the two other participants that had come in with me to place their hands on the child. I had not specifically asked what was wrong with the child, but the minute I touched her little head, I knew she had a horrible fever. Her face was flushed and her eyes were closed. I tried to keep the quiver out of my voice as I began to pray for her.

"Lord, You are the one who created this dear child. You know what the cause of her illness is and You have the power to heal her. We ask that You cause her body to begin fighting whatever the infection is. We ask that You strengthen her body. We ask that You reduce her fever. Father, we ask in the powerful name of Jesus that You heal this precious little girl. Make her well. Restore her health. Give her life. Give her the chance to know how much You love her. Father, we ask that You take our faith and multiply it—and that You answer our prayer for healing in Jesus' Name, Amen."

Have you ever wanted to just keep praying in order to give God time to work? I seriously considered adding several more

202 • JANN GRAY

paragraphs. But I realized that such a desire was more indicative of my fear that my faith wasn't enough than it was a favor to God, so I stopped. I did keep my head bowed and in the time it took to say *Amen,* I felt a peace come over my heart and mind like I had never experienced. Each of the other two participants also prayed for this little girl, with our translator sharing their words with the others in the room. During the prayer of the second participant, I felt impressed to kneel down so that I was closer to her. While keeping one hand on her head, I took her little hand in mine. At one point, I felt her squeeze my hand—it was the first indication that she could hear what we were saying or was even aware that we were there. Not only did she squeeze my hand, but she held onto it when I started to let go of her little fingers at the end of the prayer.

I knew her little body was fighting!

The doctor stepped in closer and saw that she was holding tightly to my hand. He called a nurse to come and take her temperature. The nurse stepped up and checked her temperature. I so wished I could see what it said, but I couldn't.

My interpreter told me that the nurse asked for another thermometer because she thought the one that she was using was broken. He said that it was probably broken because none of the equipment in the hospital looked like it worked. But when the second thermometer was brought, the results were the same.

Her temperature was just over 100°!

The doctor had pushed the nurse aside and was leaning down to look more closely at the little girl when she opened her eyes. We all jumped—including the doctor! He stepped back and then begin sharing with us more information about the little girl. She had come to them with a very high temperature. They didn't have any antibiotics or other medicines to combat the fever or the infection causing it. It just continued to rise and had been dangerously high for the past 24 hours. She had gone into convulsions and they had put her into ice baths to attempt to bring the fever down, but to avail. They knew her body couldn't fight whatever was making it so sick . . . and it was evident that she was going to die.

He asked the little girl a question and in a squeaky voice, she answered him. My heart was so full that I couldn't help but burst into tears as I hugged her mother and the nurse that had been caring for this sweet little girl. God had healed her body.

Praise God from whom all blessings, all healing and all answered prayers flow!

Now the doctor was anxious for our bus group to come inside and meet with the children. He also insisted that we meet with all the staff in their conference room, as he wanted all of them to know what God had done. He began the meeting by telling his staff about his challenge to us on the bus and what had happened with the little girl after we prayed for her. He then turned to me and said, "*Please tell us all how to know this Jesus whose Name is so powerful that it can heal a sick little girl in the middle of Russia!*" That day, we had more than 100 staff from the hospital pray to ask Jesus into their hearts. There were also about 70 children and their parents who accepted Christ as their Savior that day. God did a mighty work, and to him be the honor and glory!

I have prayed for healing many times since and I have seen God answer in miraculous ways. Sometimes his answer is to use medicine as part of his plan; sometimes there is no explanation for the healing other than it is God-ordained. Still, there are other times when God provides the ultimate healing and takes them home to live with him. I trust all of His answers. They are all reflections of His goodness, wisdom and power. I've never again seen Him instantaneously heal someone like He did that day, but I will never again doubt that He can!

There is power in prayer—and I know that you have sharable stories from your own life of when God answered in the way that only He can! I encourage you to share those encounters in your *Legacy Journal* project. Your encounter will encourage the hearts of those who read your testimony in the future.

Creative Walk Through Of My Entries

Let the Wise Hear – Proverbs 1:5

I chose to go two different routes on these entries. The first, I chose to use a close-up image of an ear to remind us all that an important aspect of prayer is listening. Sometimes simple is best. I've included this ear in the **One and Done Stones of Remembrance** set because it is such a great image for so many things. I did a light watercolor wash over the image and then added some shading and detail with colored pencil. I used a brush pen to add the titling.

We Will Pray Over This Child – James 5:15

For the Russian story, I knew that I had a lot of journaling to share. I chose to use the iconic matrushka dolls to visually tie the story to where it took place. I found the images with a Google search and printed them out on vellum to color and cut out. Not all tip-ins need to be attached to the edge of the page. I thought my little dolls would be the perfect place to tuck my journaling—and you might think about doing something similar in one of your own projects. I used watercolor to create a background for the dolls and then attached them with a washi tape hinge.

Inspiration

Prayer Verses:

1 Kings 8:28, 1 Kings 8:49, Nehemiah 1:11, Psalm 6:9, Psalm 17:6, Psalm 54:2, Psalm 66:19, Matthew 6:5, Matthew 21:22, Mark 11:22-25, Luke 11:2, Acts 2:42, Romans 12:12, 2 Corinthians 13:9, Philippians 1:9, Philippians 4:6, Colossians 4:2, James 5:13, James 5:15-16, 1 Peter 3:12

Listening Verses:

Proverbs 1:5, Proverbs 1:33, Proverbs 7:24, Proverbs 8:34, Proverbs 19:27

Prayer Prompts:

1. Share a story of an encounter you had with God in prayer.
2. Illustrate the Lord's Prayer with examples from your life. (Luke 11:2)
3. Write a prayer for the recipient of the Bible.
4. Record specific prayers with a date stamp next to an appropriate verse and then return and write the answer to that prayer when you receive it.

CHAPTER 17

Stacking The Stones

*You also, like living stones, are being built into a
spiritual house to be a holy priesthood, offering spiritual
sacrifices acceptable to God through Jesus Christ.*
1 Peter 2:5

You, dear reader, are a *living stone*. Your life stands as a
testimony to the faithfulness of God. You really don't know
how much I wish I could sit down with you right now and encourage you to keep offering yourself as a spiritual sacrifice
to God, just as Peter encouraged all Christ followers to do.
From the moment I began to even think about writing this
book, I have had you in my heart and on my mind . . . and I
don't want to leave you to your project until I have had a
chance to pray for you.

But we're not quite finished yet, so I need to throw away
my Kleenex and put the finishing touches on our *Stones of
Remembrance.*

When we last visited with Joshua and the people of Israel,
there were 12 burly guys lugging 12 boulders to the place
where the people were going to camp that night. They took
them to a place called Gilgal.[1] We don't know for certain
where Gilgal is, but it is most likely somewhere northeast of

modern-day Jericho. I had the opportunity to visit Israel several years ago with the Josh McDowell Ministry. The area around Jericho has a feel to it that is different from other parts of the country. There are more open spaces there and it still has a bit of a desert feel than what you will find closer to Jerusalem and Bethlehem. In those cities, it isn't uncommon to find groves of Olive trees and flocks of sheep on the hillsides. Jericho also isn't very much like the areas you find up north near the Sea of Galilee, which have a much more lush feel to them because of the natural water supplies there. Gilgal had enough space for the hundreds of thousands of people to camp, a perfect place for them to spent their first night in their new homeland.

Isn't that incredible to think about? They were *home* for the first time, and yet it was a place that none of them were familiar with . . . at all.

Do you remember the first night you spent in the place that you considered your first home? For me, it was such a night of celebration...well, and a little fear. As a missionary, I lived in lots of apartments and duplexes, but I never owned a real home until I moved to Tennessee. The day I moved in was exhausting and we didn't get much more done other than pushing all of the boxes against the walls and putting sheets on the bed. There had been so much hustle and bustle with friends helping me move boxes that I hadn't even had a single moment to myself to soak in the significance this was my new home. But then when everyone left, my sweet cocker spaniel, Anastasia, and I finally had a moment to walk into each room for the first time. And do you know what I remember most about that moment? It was so very quiet! You see, Anastasia and I had always lived in the city and you don't realize how much ambient noise you are accustomed to until you move out into the country where your neighbors are cows. I could tell that Anastasia was thinking it was awfully quiet too because she seemed to jump every time I stepped on a creaky floorboard. But we were honestly too tired to do more than have a quick snuggle, drop onto the mattress and fall sound asleep before our heads could even hit the pillow.

But our sleep didn't last long. We were awakened to the sound of someone in the bushes next to the window outside the bedroom. Anastasia was on full alert and I could tell that the motion sensor lights had been triggered because there was a sliver of light coming through the blinds. My heart started pounding and I don't mind telling you that I was more than a little scared. After traveling to all of the "dangerous" places I had been as a missionary, I thought for sure that I was going to be killed by a small town axe murderer on my first night in my new home.

And Anastasia wasn't helping matters. She was doing her "whisper growl," which she initiated any time she wanted to get my attention without anyone else noticing. She probably thought she was saying, *"Hey Mom, don't look now . . . I said don't look! But I think there is someone very scary on the other side of that window!"* I got up, knowing that there was nothing I could find to use as a weapon. But clearly, Anastasia thought one of us needed to check out what was going on— and it wasn't going to be her!

I made my way in the dark towards the window, navigating around the piles of boxes. I pushed apart a couple of the mini blinds to see if I could catch a glimpse of who was there, who obviously intended to do us harm. And staring back at me was a doe...a deer...a female deer. The look she was giving me very clearly asked, "What are you doing on our property!" I laughed with relief and told Anastasia that we were going to live to see another day because it wasn't an axe murderer, rather it was one of our neighbors who had just dropped by to say hello and welcome us to the neighborhood. We both fell back into bed and went fast asleep once again, home at last. By the way, those deer still walk down the driveway every night…they just don't wake us up anymore. Apparently, we're country folk now!

But that first night at Gilgal was probably filled with a little bit of anxiety for the people of Israel too. They had been wandering so long that they had forgotten what it was like to have a home. They knew that they faced neighbors who weren't going to be thrilled that they had moved into the neighborhood. They knew that God had promised this place to them as a homeland, but they were uncertain what it would actually be like to live there. So I love that God chose that place to have them set up their memorial—their stones of remembrance!

God is Master of the details. Joshua 4:19 tells us that it was the tenth day of the first month when they crossed the Jordan and made camp. That was the very day that they were to begin preparing the Passover celebration initiated by God back in Egypt. It was the very day that they were to select the lamb that was to be sacrificed for the Passover meal.[2] Isn't that just too wonderful? It was the blood of the Passover Lamb that made it possible for them to leave Egypt with their firstborn sons still alive, while the sons of all the Egyptians, including Pharaoh's, had been killed. It was time to select the Passover Lamb once again. God had brought them home on the very day He had set aside for them to remember His deliverance. And on that special day, He asked them to build a permanent memorial from the stones they had taken from the riverbed. That attention to detail just makes me love Him all the more! He knew that they were going to have battles to fight in order to make this promised land their homeland, so He was reminding them once again that He had brought them this far—and He would be with them until the end.

So they stacked their stones. Joshua told the people of Israel that they were to use these stones as opportunities to start conversations with their children. They were to say that God had them prepare this memorial so that *"all the people of the earth might know that the hand of the Lord is powerful and so you might always fear the Lord your God."*[3]

It's time for you to begin stacking your own stones of remembrance. I believe that what you will accomplish for your family is right in line with to the reasons God commanded Joshua to stack high those stones from the Jordan River. And I believe that He will be with you as you do so, just as He was with Joshua and the people of Israel.

I'm really not ready for us to be done with our time together, but nevertheless, the time has come. I can't say goodbye without praying over you the same prayer that I have offered for you every day as I have sat down to write.

Heavenly Father,

I pray and lay hold of Your promise that "no eye has seen, nor ear heard, nor the heart of man imagined what [You] have prepared for those who love [You].[4]
Bless this dear one. Let them feel Your presence as they begin to prepare their own Stones of Remembrance project to document Your faithfulness in their lives and the lives of the people whom they love. Refresh their spirits and renew their minds. Give them creative ideas to express the love they have for You in their hearts on the pages of this Bible . . . and give

them confidence that You will guide them each step of the way.

Lord, I also pray for each person who will receive one of these special gifts. I ask that You prepare their hearts to receive it—and help them to view this gift as a reflection of Your powerful hand so that it will cause them to love You more and serve You better for the remainder of their lives.

Thank You for sending Your Son to die for them!

Thank You for leaving Your Spirit to live in them!

Thank You for allowing me to touch their lives on Your behalf! You have made it clear how much You love them...and You have placed a love in my heart for them too.

I ask that You bless them and keep them. May Your face shine upon them and give them peace.

Amen

Notes

[1] Joshua 4:20, New International Version, Thomas Nelson Publishers.
[2] Exodus 12:3, New Living Translation, Tyndale House Publishers.
[3] Joshua 4:24, New International Version, Thomas Nelson Publishers.
[4] 1 Corinthians 2:9, English Standard Version, Crossway Bible Publishers

About The Author

Jann Gray is an innovative writer, marketer, designer and speaker with more than three decades of experience in ministry! ***Stones of Remembrance*** is her second book focusing on Bible Journaling. Her first book, ***Illuminated Journaling***, was the flagship book in the Bible Journaling movement and continues to help beginning Bible journalers begin their own journey of responding creatively to God's Word. Because Jann knows that adding imagery onto the pages of a Bible can be a bit intimidating, she has developed a line of products to help even the most nervous journaler be successful right from the start. Her line art products called ***One and Dones*** and **Click Prints** provide a quick and easy way to add artwork onto whatever surface a journaler chooses.

Jann lives in Nashville, Tennessee but travels several weeks each month to speak and teach at Christian conferences, women's retreats, art studios, churches and bookstores. Her enthusiasm is infectious and she has developed a strong following via social media, her website, live events and on-line workshops, as well as her more than 200 free tutorials offered on YouTube.

Let's Stay In Touch

I want to stay in touch and I hope you do too!

Please visit my website and discover all the resources that I have available there to help you on your journey of personal *Bible Journaling* or *Legacy Journaling.*

www.IlluminatedJournaling.com

Some of the resources you will find there are:
- Free Tutorials
- On-line Workshops
- Bible Journaling Products
- Newsletter
- Calendar Of Events
- Links To My Social Media Accounts

I would love to hear from you. Please feel free to contact me at Jann@JannGray.com! I get some of my best inspiration from you—so don't hesitate to let me know how I can help!

Finally, if you would like to book me for a live event, please contact Royce at 615-773-1234.